Contents

Foreword

BY REGGIE MCNEAL

"IF THE SALVATION ARMY didn't exist, God would have to create it." I often use these words as my opening lines when speaking to an assembly of Salvationists. I don't say this to be nice; I really mean it!

Why do I feel this way? In my estimation I believe The Salvation Army is uniquely positioned to call the party for advancing God's kingdom in every community where the Army has an expression. God's kingdom has always been his major concern, so any group that co-conspires with him on his agenda has missional alignment with what God is up to in the world. The resulting reality is that kingdom-centric people and organizations are in position to receive and invest kingdom resources. In other words, they become sluice gates for the kingdom of God to flow through into this world. They function as answers to the petition we've been taught to pray, that the kingdom would "come on earth as it is in heaven."

If one understands what the kingdom of God is all about it becomes apparent as to why I think The Salvation Army serves as an agent of this kingdom. I like to explain the kingdom of God as "life as God intends." Life is the point of the kingdom. The Bible bears strong witness to this truth. It opens its narrative in a garden with the Tree of Life at its center. It closes out in a city with the River of Life flowing through its center, lined with trees of Life on both banks.

Jesus emphasized this theme not only by saying that he came to give us life, but that he *is* the Life itself! Since Jesus tied his own life and ministry to the kingdom of God (over ninety times in the four Gospels he refers to the kingdom) it is obvious that he thought that the point of it all is life. And his life and ministry embodied the kingdom, gaining spiritual access to spiritual life for us all, but also along the way healing the sick and raising the dead. In other words, Jesus not only pointed out the life God intends (spiritually, physically, emotionally, etc.) but he actually lived the Life for us to see. He truly is the only complete Human Being ever to walk the planet.

Here's where The Salvation Army gets in this picture. It preaches and teaches the kingdom of God. But it also embodies this message, helping people have a shot at the life God intends for them by tending to their needs across the board—spiritual, material, and emotional. This kingdom-centric agenda is what makes the Army essential to the world.

But The Salvation Army is also essential to the church, particularly the Western church in its current state of missional amnesia.

When Jesus established the church he never intended for it to usurp the kingdom as God's primary concern on planet earth. The church was created against the backdrop of the kingdom to bear witness to the kingdom. Only to the extent that the church plays its proper role in respect to the kingdom does it live out its mission. The world is supposed to be pointed to the kingdom by the church, not confused by some message that the church is the biggest thing God has going on the planet. The Western church-as-institution increasingly has become self-absorbed and self-promoting, with the kingdom message being marginalized. The culture's disaffection with the church-centric narrative is well deserved and should call us to repentance and realignment with God's story—the saga of the kingdom.

The Salvation Army can help the Western church know the way out of the wilderness as it:

- Serves people's needs across all areas of life;

- Addresses people's needs without requiring them to become church people;

- Advocates for the least and the lost;

- Synergizes cross-domain efforts to move the needle on big societal issues;

- Celebrates a scorecard that is life-centric, bigger than the typical church scorecard that measures church activity.

Out of Australia comes this volume you are reading. I am not surprised. My engagement with them over the past years has introduced me to a group of spiritual leaders who are eager and courageously committed to being the people of God. They believe that the kingdom helps people find freedom, and they are putting their lives where their hopes are.

If you are a Salvationist I hope this book reignites your passion for the movement you are a part of. If you are someone like me—outside the Army but an admirer—I hope the book encourages you to be a viral kingdom agent and a champion for church-as-movement where you have influence.

I hope God uses this discussion to help us be even more his people of blessing so that the kingdom can more easily pour through us, so that people can experience the life that God intends for them.

Because life *is* the point.

Reggie McNeal, author of *Kingdom Come and Missional Renaissance.*

Preface

We met some years ago when we were both teaching Introduction to Mission at our respective training colleges in Australia. We quickly sensed we were on the same page when it came to missional ideas and were keen to share ideas and resources. One of our burning questions was "what textbook are you using"? We had both struggled to find the ideal book to share with our students and that is where the idea of writing this book was born. It took another eight years till we found ourselves in a position to start working on that dream. Since that time some great new books are on the market and we feel more spoilt for choice with great missional resources than ever. However, we still felt there was a need to hear missional thinking from the perspective of The Salvation Army. We don't offer this book as people with academic or biblical pedigrees, but throughout these pages we will refer you to people we believe can share from that perspective. We offer this book as thoughtful practitioners. We have been involved in frontline ministry and also in teaching mission. This book is the result of those experiences. We trust it will help you as you think and live missionally in your context today.

Lynette and Gregory

Acknowledgments

In a book about partnering with God, it is only fitting that we thank those who partnered with us to make this project a reality.

To Donald Burke, Sue Smartt, and Colin Reynolds, who read our first attempts at expressing ourselves and gave invaluable feedback. This project is so much better thanks to you.

To those who contributed the stories, or snapshots, which illustrate our thoughts. Thank you for sharing your experience. This project is richer for your contributions.

To our students over the years who have taught us so much, the project owes its genesis and inspiration to you.

Finally, to Aged Care Plus, The Salvation Army, Australia. We owe you a great debt of gratitude for your belief in our project and financial support to make it a reality. This project would not have been possible without you.

Introduction

FINDING A TITLE FOR our book proved to be one of the more challenging aspects of this project. At one time the front-runner was *Vision Splendid*. This name was a reference to the song by Doris Rendell which captured something of the message of our book.

> We have caught the vision splendid
> Of a world which is to be,
> When the pardoning love of Jesus
> Freely flows from sea to sea,
> When all men from strife and anger,
> Greed and selfishness are free,
> When the nations live together
> In sweet peace and harmony.
>
> We would help to build the city
> Of our God, so wondrous fair;
> Give our time, bring all our talents,
> And each gift of beauty rare,
> Powers of mind, and strength of purpose,
> Days of labour, nights of strain,
> That God's will may be accomplished,
> O'er the kingdoms he shall reign.[1]

We believe that Christian mission is God's work to bring about the new creation. We are invited to partner with God in that most remarkable of tasks. The title we chose in the end says this more plainly. We are invited

---

1. Rendell, *Song Book*, 938.

into a profound partnership with God, bringing about the world as it was intended to be. This is mission, God's kingdom come here and now and also in the future.

God's kingdom come is broad and all encompassing. It is a mission big enough for all to find a place. However this book is most specifically interested in the place of The Salvation Army in that great adventure. We are an organization who was once called the Christian Mission. With the passage of time that name was removed from our masthead, but it is our sincere hope and prayer that it is never moved from our DNA. This book is our contribution to keeping mission the focus of our movement and our lives.

We see the word mission being used more and more recently. It appears in organizational job titles, department names, tasks and roles. We even risk losing the meaning and focus of mission through dilution. This is all the more reason for us as The Salvation Army to identify what mission really means and how we live it out in our day, our context.

We, the authors, are Australians and are offering this book and our insights from a Western, and indeed an Australian perspective. While we share some stories from across the globe, it is important for us to clarify that we do not feel qualified to speak about mission from the perspective of the Global South; there are people from those countries far more capable than we are for that task.[2] Our insights are shaped by our contexts here in Australia and in countries with which we share a cultural heritage.

This book has been set out in two sections. In the first section, we will explore how to think missionally. Stories shape us. They forge our identity and influence how we act in the world. In this section of the book we will tell five key stories which have shaped us as the people of God and specifically, The Salvation Army. The first two stories are theological and biblical. The grand narratives of the Scriptures are a critical place for us to start. The following three chapters tell the stories of the church and our particular corner of it. We trace how mission was lived out in the church since the first century before telling our own story of The Salvation Army in particular. We finish section 1 with an overview story of the global church today.

The second section of this book addresses how we live those missional stories. Each chapter offers insights into one dimension of living the mission of God. Each chapter is about being. These chapters include small snapshots of how others are living out this aspect of mission within the

---

2. For excellent global perspectives see the work of Graham Hill and the Global Church Project.

Salvation Army today. Finally we offer a toolbox with some resources or ideas to apply each topic in your ministry contexts.

Doris Rendell's song suggests and vision and a response. The vision is a world which is to be. A world where peace, justice, and freedom reign. The response is that we are invited to help build that city. Here and now and into the future. It is our hope and prayer that this book might encourage and inspire us as we partner with God for God's kingdom come in our time and place.

SECTION ONE

Thinking Mission

CHAPTER ONE

Theological Story

Introduction

Have you heard people say, "Well, I'm no theologian but . . ."? Often this sentence is followed by some discussion about God and faith. Despite the person's protestations this is a theological discussion. Whenever we speak about God we are engaged in theology. Our theology is our talk, *logos*, about God, *theos*. In this opening chapter, we are going to talk about God in the context of mission. Mission asks why are we here, what is God doing in the world, and how do the gospel, culture, and church connect? To set the scene for the rest of the book we will start by outlining a theology of mission for a contemporary world.

Missio Dei: The Mission of God

A sound missional theology calls for a fresh understanding of mission as belonging to God, not us. This is *missio Dei*. *Missio Dei* is the conviction that Christian mission has its origins in the heart of God. "It is not the church that has a mission of salvation to fulfill in the world; it is the mission of the Son and the Spirit through the Father that includes the church."[1] Mission is not an activity or program. Mission is not something we do in order to bring people into the church. We talk about going on a mission trip,

---

1. Moltmann, *Church in the Power of the Spirit*, 64.

starting a mission program or asking for help from the mission department. This can lead to thinking that the church has a mission and as Christians we get involved in that missional activity. However, this understanding of mission is mistaken. Mission is God's sending heart. It is not something we have to initiate and accomplish but rather something we are invited to join. We are offered the opportunity to partner with God in the world. This mission is to redeem all peoples and, in fact, all of creation for God's self. The church is invited to be part of that great task. "Understanding mission as God-centric not church centric reframes our understanding completely. Mission is the result of God's initiative, rooted in God's purposes to restore and heal creation."[2] The shift to understanding mission as God's mission and not ours is of Copernican dimensions. It changes everything.[3]

God is already at work in the world. God is missionary in nature. Understanding mission from the perspective of *missio Dei* invites us to look for where God is working in the world and join him there. When we understand this, our focus changes from bringing "unchurched" people in, to sending Christian people out. Sometimes we have relied entirely upon an attractional mission model. We set ourselves up in our little corner called the church and we invite people to come and join us here. *Missio Dei* is based upon the central notion of being sent. God is a sending God. Sending language is threaded throughout the full story of Scripture. God is always sending and this sending is always purposeful. God takes the initiative.

This idea of the sending God is born from the Trinity. "The classical doctrine of the *missio Dei* as God the Father sending the Son, and God the Father and the Son sending the Spirit was expanded to include yet another 'movement': Father, Son and the Holy Spirit sending the church into the world. As far as missionary thinking was concerned, this linking with the doctrine of the Trinity constituted an important innovation."[4] The Greek word *perichoresis* is often used to express the relationship between each person in the godhead. It expresses the concept of mutual indwelling. Contained in this word are the words *peri*, meaning around, and *chorein,* which among other things, means to make room for. The persons of the godhead dwell in *perichoretic* union. They dance together, make room for the other, and indwell one another. Misoslav Volf has eloquently argued that it is the very

2. Van Gelder, *Missional Church*, 6.

3. Ott, *Encountering Theology of Mission*, 62.

4. Bosch, *Transforming Mission*, 400.

essence of God, of divinity, to include the other.[5] In his third book, *After Our Likeness*, he encourages us to find our missional identity in the Trinity itself. Created in the image of the triune God we cannot but be missional.[6]

Throughout Scripture God was sending. Sometimes sending people such as prophets or angels, and sometimes sending through acts of nature. God the Father sent the Son and the Spirit. Jesus concluded his earthly ministry by sending his disciples. The word apostle, in Greek, *apostolos*, means "one who is sent away." In John 20:21 Jesus said, "As the Father has sent me, I am sending you." Later in Acts 1:7–9 Jesus hands over his mission to his disciples and sends them into the world as his emissaries. The ascension is a key missiological text of the sending God at work, in and through his followers.

This emphasis on being a sent people does not negate the significance of also being a gathered people. In a later chapter, we will explore the power and value of the gathered community, specifically as they gather for worship. Nor does the emphasis on being a sent people mean we are not called also to be an attractive community. Wright has said that "God's mission involves God's people living in God's way in the sight of the nations."[7] As we live in sight of the nations our calling is to be an attractive and compelling community. We are to demonstrate the beauty of the kingdom of God in action. Being sent does not contradict being attractive, attractional or gathered, but it does supplant them as the central call. Being sent is our primal stance in the world.

So far, we have argued that mission belongs to God and we are invited to join in that mission in the world and creation. God is a sending God and we, by extension, are sent people. As his followers today, we are invited into this journey. God is active and we, the church, "must run to catch up with what God is already doing in the world."[8]

There is a lovely illustration of this in *The Chronicles of Narnia* where we meet the Pevensie children—Peter, Susan, Edmund and Lucy—who encounter the wonderful world of Narnia and also the god-like figure, the great lion Aslan. In *Prince Caspian*, the children are brought back to Narnia to help Prince Caspian defeat his uncle Miraz, who had usurped the throne. The children set out once again to save Narnia. They jump straight into the quest

---

5. Volf, *Exclusion and Embrace*.

6. Volf, *After Our Likeness*.

7. Wright, *Mission of God*, 470.

8. Cox, *God's Revolution and Man's Responsibility*, 24.

using their own skill and ingenuity but Lucy isn't happy with this plan. She suggests instead that they wait till they see Aslan and seek his advice before heading off. The other children decide to get on with their task in the hope that Aslan might turn up along the way. After quite some time, they come to a vast ravine and it is then that Lucy sees Aslan. He seems to signal that she should follow him, in the opposite direction to that which the children had planned. However, the other children are unconvinced that she has even seen him. In the movie version of this scene Peter asks Lucy why Aslan only revealed himself to her and not to the rest of the group. She responds beautifully by suggesting "perhaps you weren't looking for him."

Maybe there are times when we do not have our eyes open looking for God in our daily lives. God is active in the world. What amazing God-sightings and God-promptings would we see if we had our eyes and hearts open?

Salvation

There are many interconnected theological concepts which are part of the rich tapestry of missional thinking and living. *Missio Dei* is vital as it rightly positions mission as belonging to God. Another key concept is that of salvation, which is concerned with the nature and scope of God's work in the world. Those of us associated with The Salvation Army use this theological term on a daily basis, every time we say our name. It is possible that we have not stopped to think deeply about what we mean by it or how is shapes our lives. However, it is important as our understanding of salvation shapes our missiology and our missiological engagement.

Salvation is a central idea in most religions and is based on the idea that the world in general and us as individuals are not as we should be. Through salvation we are invited to redemption, to fullness of living, to be all that we were intended to be. The academic study of salvation is called soteriology. In Scripture, the ideas of salvation are broad and holistic. Salvation is for this world and the next, for individuals and communities, for the earth as well as humanity. The Hebrew Bible characterizes salvation as "'material'—that is, concerned with lived, concrete, socio-political issues [as opposed to] . . . frequent Christian claims that salvation is something spiritual and otherworldly. In reality, the Old Testament knows no such dualism as material-spiritual, and regards every aspect of life—personal and public, present and future—as open to YHWH's saving capacity. Thus 'salvation' is deliverance from any and every circumstance and any negative power that prevents full, joyous, communal existence."[9]

Themes of a broad and embracing salvation continue in the New Testament. Numerous times in Luke's gospel Jesus is heard saying "your faith has saved you" (Luke 7:50; 8:48; 17:19; 18:42) and on each occasion salvation is both present and holistic. Not only was the salvation about physical healing, but also heralded access to social, religious and community life. Luke uses salvation to describe the renewal of the whole of human life, its economic, physical, political, and religious dimensions.[10] One of the iconic hymns of The Salvation Army is the Founders Song, with the words "O boundless salvation, Deep ocean of love"[11] and this boundless nature of salvation is critical to an accurate missional theology.

There is some feeling today that the church is suffering from "soteriological shrinkage"[12] or "soteriological self-centeredness."[13] This argument suggests we have narrowed our understanding of salvation from its broad beauty into something limited and inadequate. We have come to understand salvation as being personal and individual. Some have made it even smaller than the individual person and talk about saving the souls of people only. Further we have limited our salvation to being future focused and about getting into heaven when we die. Sadly, salvation is sometimes understood as simply an escape route for individual people from this world to the next. Willard has provocatively suggested that this limited view of salvation "produces vampire Christians who want Jesus for his blood and little else."[14]

Throughout the New Testament "salvation was bound up with the coming of the kingdom of God, the restoration of God's rule over all human life and all of creation."[15] This paints a picture of the full scope of the Christian salvation we enjoy and share with each other, the world and the cosmos.

9. Brueggemann, *Reverberations of Faith*, 185.

10. Goheen, *Introducing Christian Mission*, 90.

11. Booth, *Songbook*, 509.

12. Davies-Kildea, *Unwrapping Our Bounded Salvation*, 2.

13. Goheen, *Introducing Christian Mission*, 91.

14. Willard, *Divine Conspiracy*, 403.

15. Goheen, *Introducing Christian Mission*, 90.

Kingdom of God

In the context of God's activity in the world and its scope of boundless salvation we come to another key concept, the kingdom of God. The kingdom of God was Jesus' central message. In Mark 1:15 we hear Jesus saying, "The time has come. . . . The kingdom of God has come near. Repent and believe the good news!" In Matthew 6:10 Jesus guides his followers to pray God's kingdom come.[16] Theologian John Bright wrote, "The Bible is one book. Had we to give that book a title we might with justice call it 'The Book of the Coming Kingdom of God.' That is indeed its central theme everywhere."[17] The kingdom of God speaks of the reign of God, his kingly rule. It is a realm not a place, spiritual not geographical. The kingdom of God is a sphere where God's rule is accepted in the lives of people, or even more simply, where life is lived as God intended. In Genesis, we see a picture of the first creation where all things, people and creation, lived in harmony and the *shalom* of God was realized. We do not need the narrative of Genesis to know that we do not live in such a world now. Instead we are working towards and looking forward to the new creation when such an order is restored. The biblical story is a grand narrative arranged around the plotline of creation, fall, redemption and restoration.[18] We are invited to be part of the journey towards the world as God intended it through how we act and what we say. "Mission is both the announcement and the demonstration of the reign of God through Christ."[19] This means that mission is not focused on the growth of the church but on God's kingdom and how that might be expressed and lived out today. "What constitutes the mission of the church? It has to do with partnering with God as his people in his mission. That mission is the kingdom of God, not the church. Jesus told us to pray, 'Thy kingdom come,' not, 'Thy church come.' Though the church plays a vital role in the kingdom, it is not the point of the kingdom."[20]

The kingdom is come through both words and deeds. Binaries here are unhelpful, talking about either/or is not constructive. The kingdom of God encompasses social action *and* spoken word, service *and* evangelism,

16. Matthew primarily uses the term "kingdom of heaven" and other gospel writers use the term "kingdom of God." The majority of theologians recognize the terms as synonymous.

17. Bright, *Kingdom of God*, 197.

18. Wright, *Mission of God*, 63.

19. Frost, *Road to Missional*, 24.

20. McNeal, *Kingdom Come*, 8.

practical help *and* pronouncement. The World Evangelical Fellowship in 1983 stated that the "mission of the church includes both proclamation of the Gospel and its demonstration."[21] We are given many glimpses into what this kingdom might look like here on earth. It will be a place of welcome and diversity (Matt 8:11; 22:2–10), it will be a place of enough (Matt 6:25–33), it will be a place of healing and joy (Rev 21:1–14), it is penetrating and expanding (Matt 13:31–33).

Michael Frost suggests a metaphor which is very helpful in living out the kingdom of God here and now. He invites us to imagine the world to come, when the world is regenerated as it was intended to be. Then think of that as the biggest blockbuster movie of all time. Our lives, both collectively and individually, are to be like a preview of that upcoming feature.

> The church is to be like a trailer for the New Jerusalem, a taster, with all the best bits on full display. If we conclude that the world to come will be a place of complete and perfect justice it follows that the mission of the church is to create foretastes of the justice that is to come. Likewise, if we believe that the world to come is a place of love and mercy, we are to be a trailer of that love and mercy, a free sample for those looking to buy into the whole thing. Read the Scriptures and compile a picture of the world to come— justice love, peace, reconciliation—and then go forth to fashion foretastes of that world.[22]

Followers of Jesus are invited to pray "Thy kingdom come" with our eyes and hearts open to how we might be part of the answer to that prayer. We could pray Thy kingdom come, Thy will be done in my community as it is in heaven. As N. T. Wright beautifully states, "What you do in the present—by painting, preaching, singing, sewing, praying, teaching building hospitals, digging wells, campaigning for justice, writing poems, caring for the needy, loving your neighbor as yourself—will last into God's future. These activities are not simply ways of making the present life a little less beastly, a little more bearable, until the day when we leave it behind altogether. . . . They are part of what we may call building for God's kingdom."[23]

---

21. Bosch, *Transforming Mission*, 417.

22. Frost, *Road to Missional*, 29.

23. Wright, *Surprised by Hope*, 193.

Incarnation

If kingdom living can be understood as life as God intended it to be, then the incarnation offers us a window into that world. The incarnation is the demonstration of the universality of God "played out within history in particularity."[24] When trying to understand the incarnation Philip Yancey offers a metaphor. Imagine a person who keeps tropical fish in a tank. The human who cares for the fish puts great effort, time and money into ensuring the well-being and survival of the fish, but the fish are unable to even conceive of the being who does all this. Instead, every time a human hand enters the tank they dart around in fear. There is only one way for the incomprehensible to become comprehensible to the fish. The human would need to become a fish and enter the tank.[25] This might help us grasp something so much bigger and more complex. In the incarnation, the divine takes on human form and comes as one we can begin to understand.

While the doctrine of the incarnation has primarily focused on the person and work of Jesus, incarnation also appears throughout the Hebrew Bible. In Isa 7:14 and Isa 8:8 we hear of *Imman-él*, the "with us God." The Hebrew Bible is the story of God's self-disclosure to humanity that becomes focused in and for the people of Israel. While God is always present in the world, there are particular intensifying moments of divine presences that we call theophany. "In fact, theophany suggests that the finite (creation) is capable of the infinite. God can come and be present in storm, pillar of cloud and fire. God can appear in the human form of the *mal'ak*. The world can serve the task of clothing God."[26] So throughout the Hebrew Bible we experience God as one who "can temporarily incarnate himself."[27]

In the person of Jesus, we see the incarnation of God in its fullest expression. God made human. Possibly the verse which sums this up for us most powerfully is John 1:14: "The word became flesh and made his dwelling among us. We have seen his glory, the glory of the one and only, who came from the Father, full of grace and truth." Incarnation literally means, "in the flesh" and primarily refers to the Divine taking on human nature and becoming fully human. In the year 451 this doctrine was expressed in a creed we have come to know as the Chalcedon Creed. "Following, then,

24. Ott, *Encountering Theology of Mission*, 59.

25. Yancey, *Jesus I Never Knew*, 38.

26. Fretheim, *Suffering of God*, 92.

27. Eichrodt, *Theology of the Old Testament*, 27.

the holy Fathers, we all unanimously teach that our Lord Jesus Christ is to us One and the same Son, the Self-same Perfect in Godhead, the Self-same Perfect in Manhood; truly God and truly Man."[28] The salvation of humankind is to be found in the whole scope of the incarnation. Jesus' life, death, resurrection and ascension were all expressions of the "with us God."

The incarnation of Christ is not only an event of salvific value, it also indicates a paradigm of how God chooses to work in the world. Incarnational ministry describes that mode of missionary engagement that takes its cue from the doctrine of the incarnation of God in Christ. "Christ's incarnation has become one of the most widely used motifs in conceptualizing mission."[29] We must urge caution that we are not suggesting that we are able to emulate the Divine experience. The mystery of incarnation in the Christian faith is unique to God's action alone. Nor are we encouraging a form of colonialism whereby we condescend to enter another's world. Rather, through the incarnation we are offered a model of empathy and profound identification in our missional encounters. Incarnation offers a motif to shape our missional engagement.

The Message translation offers us this rendering of John 1:14: "The Word became flesh and blood, and moved into the neighborhood. We saw the glory with our own eyes, the one-of-a-kind glory, like Father, like Son, Generous inside and out, true from start to finish." What a great line, *God moved into the neighborhood*, our neighborhood, the community we live in: God intimate and engaged.

God's preferred way of engaging with the world was the model of incarnation. Those of us who follow his lead are likewise called to choose incarnation as our primary missional model. This model calls us to contextualize the gospel in our culture and context. Paul demonstrates this model of mission in Acts 17. He spent time understanding the context, presented the claims of Christ with respect, he used the methods of that culture and was open to dialogue. He summarizes his approach in 1 Cor 9:20–22: "To the Jews I became like a Jew, to win the Jews. To those under the law I became like one under the law (though I myself am not under the law), so as to win those under the law. To those not having the law I became like one not having the law (though I am not free from God's law but am under Christ's law), so as to win those not having the law. To the weak I became

---

28. Leith, *Creeds of the Churches*, 35

29. Ott, *Encountering Theology of Mission*, 97.

weak, to win the weak. I have become all things to all people so that by all possible means I might save some."

The Lausanne Conference Manila Manifesto says, "Our continuing commitment to social action is not a confusion of the kingdom of God with a Christianized society. It is, rather, a recognition that the biblical gospel has inescapable social implications. *True mission should always be incarnational.* It necessitates entering humbly into other people's worlds, identifying with their social reality, their sorrow and suffering, and their struggles for justice against oppressive powers."[30]

So far in this chapter we have explored three key concepts. In the *missio Dei* we understand that Christians are sent people. The kingdom of God gives purpose to our "sent-ness" as we demonstrate the world as God intended it to be and the incarnation offers a model of how we should engage in that mission. We are invited to profound connection, to deep relationship, to genuine identification, and engagement.

Imago Dei

Another foundational idea in our missional theology is *imago Dei*. I suspect the idea of being created in the image of God sounds familiar to you. In Gen 1:27 we are told that humans were created in the image of God and in 2 Cor 3:18 that we "are being transformed into the same image from glory to glory, even as from the Lord Spirit." From these verses, among others, comes this idea that we are God's image bearers, which is unique to the relationship between God and humanity. "The concept of the *imago Dei* has been widely recognized as central to a Christian understanding of human beings, yet the paucity of biblical references has left the way open for a wide variety of philosophical and theological interpretations of this notion."[31]

So, what does it mean to bear the image of God in humanity? There are three main ways this has been interpreted. First, as functional. Humanity has been entrusted with the role of being responsible over the rest of God's creation. Second, ontologically, which refers to the nature of humanity. This might be demonstrated through humanity's endowment with specific attributes or characteristics, such as free will or intellect, which bestow a special dignity on humanity. Third, relational. Humanity has the capacity for relationships towards God and empathy and responsibility towards others.

---

30. Lausanne Movement, "Manila Manifesto," lines 208–13 (italics added).
31. Middleton, "Liberating Image?," 8–9.

Each of these interpretations bring something to our understanding of the *imago Dei*. However, of central importance is that the *imago Dei* call humanity to be God's image bearers in the world. We are God's agents or representatives on this earth. Our likeness to God is both an inestimable treasure and also a weighty responsibility. It confers on us a glorious task as we work to see God's will be done on earth as in heaven. It also calls us to treat others as image bearers. In a later chapter, we explore this idea further as we consider the Wesleyan belief that the first word in how we view others is this: you are an image bearer of God and as such a person of infinite worth and value.

Imago Dei serves as a motivation to treat all people with dignity and respect. If all are of value, then we must act in ways which ensure justice and equality for all. Think about how that impacts our interactions with others. That child is an image bearer of God. That elderly person is an image bearer of God. That annoying coworker, obnoxious family member, or violent prisoner. We are called to treat all people with dignity and worth. If we embrace the concepts of *imago Dei* then a good question for reflection is, did I treat everyone today as if that were true.

C. S. Lewis said:

> There are no *ordinary* people. You have never talked to a mere mortal. Nations, cultures, arts, civilization—these are mortal, and their life is to ours as the life of a gnat. But it is immortals whom we joke with, work with, marry, snub, and exploit—immortal horrors or everlasting splendors. This does not mean that we are to be perpetually solemn. We must play. But our merriment must be of that kind (and it is, in fact, the merriest kind) which exists between people who have, from the outset, taken each other seriously—no flippancy, no superiority, no presumption. And our charity must be real and costly love, with deep feeling for the sins in spite of which we love the sinner—no mere tolerance or indulgence which parodies love as flippancy parodies merriment. Next to the Blessed Sacrament itself, your neighbor is the holiest object presented to your senses.[32]

Imago Dei shapes our encounters with others. It shapes our response to the world. Our work towards justice, beauty, love and grace are works of great theological importance in the *missio Dei*.

32. Lewis, *Weight of Glory*, 45–46.

Justice and Shalom

This brings us to the final theme of this chapter, justice and *shalom*. In the second section of this book we will consider how to live the mission of justice and social engagement. However, first we will explore a few theological principles on which to build our later considerations.

Many Christians can recite Micah 6:8: "He has shown you, O mortal, what is good. And what does the Lord require of you? To act justly and to love mercy and to walk humbly with your God." This well-known verse expresses something of our commitment to a faith which is not only personal but communal. Justice and mercy walk hand in hand and shape our responses in the world. In the past, and to some extent still in the present, there have been debates about the either/or relationship of evangelism and social action. A holistic understanding of the gospel may be summed up in the official statement of the World Evangelical Fellowship quoted earlier, which stated that the "mission of the church includes both proclamation of the Gospel and its demonstration . . . as evil is not only in the human heart but also in social structures."[33]

Justice may be understood simply, yet profoundly, as what love looks like in action. Alternatively, it is "what love looks like in public."[34] There is no mission without justice. A deep social conscience and a "life poured out in service to others, especially the poor, is the inevitable sign of real true justifying gospel faith."[35] Working for justice might be considered an inevitable outcome of a relationship with God.

Justice is a multifaceted concept. In his book *Pursuing Justice*, Wytsma helps explain biblical justice using the image of a mosaic.

> If you wrested a shard of glass from its setting in a beautiful mosaic, took it home and placed it on the table and declared to anyone in earshot, "This is a magnificent piece of art!" . . . No matter how lovely that single shard was it in no way captures the glory of the whole. And yet often our treatment of justice is a mere single shard treatment: Justice is like a mosaic. It's not only about single pieces; it's about all the pieces working together in a stunning whole. All too often we believe that our desire to pursue justice can only be lived out or understood in a single shard. Criminal justice. International development. Creation care. Education. Anti-trafficking.

33. Bosch, *Transforming Mission*, 417.
34. Popularly attributed to Dr. Cornel West.
35. Keller, *Generous Justice*, 99.

Works of mercy and love. All of these shards are vital parts of God's mosaic of justice.[36]

There are a variety of words in the Hebrew and Greek which are variously translated as justice in our English Bibles. I'd like to introduce you to three of those words which form part of our mosaic of justice.

The first is *mishpat* which is linked to the notion of treating others equitably, of giving others what they are due. This word appears more than two hundred times in the Hebrew Bible and is most often translated as justice. It carries the sense of acquitting or punishing every person on the merits of the case, regardless of race or social status. Its most basic meaning is to treat people equitably. Leviticus 24:22 warns Israel to "have the same *mishpat* [rule of law] for the foreigner as the native." *Mishpat* is giving people what they are due, whether punishment or protection or care. Zechariah gives us this prophetic call to *mishpat*. "This is what the Lord Almighty said: administer true justice; show mercy and compassion to one another. Do not oppress the widow or the fatherless, the foreigner or the poor. Do not plot evil against each other" (Zech 7:9–10). This sort of justice is but part of the full picture. A friend of mine is the manager of a drug and alcohol rehabilitation center in which many of the participants have hurt others or even broken the law. He recommends that the residents do not ask for justice as they might not like what they receive. Instead he suggests they should ask for mercy. Our picture of justice needs to be broader than simply *mishpat*, it needs to be enlarged by mercy.

So, our mosaic is enhanced with our second Hebrew word *tzadeqah*. This refers to a life of right relationships. While sometimes translated as being just, it is usually translated as being righteous. *Tzadeqah* is a life in which all relationships, human to human, human to God, and human to creation are well ordered and harmonious. As this word is often translated as *righteousness*, it is easy for a modern reader to think in terms of private morality or devotion. However, this word *tzadeqah* is more concerned with day-to-day living. It calls us to have relationships which are shaped by generosity and equity, whether those relationships are private or civic. Alec Motyer defines the righteous as those "right with God and therefore committed to putting right all other relationships in life."[37]

---

36. Wytsma, *Pursuing Justice*, 6.
37. Motyer, *Prophecy of Isaiah*, 471.

It is not surprising to discover that *tzadeqah* and *mishpat* are juxtaposed often throughout Scripture. In Job, we see how just living looks in practice when these two principles are woven together.

> I rescued the poor who cried for help,
>> and the fatherless who had none to assist them.
> The one who was dying blessed me;
>> I made the widow's heart sing.
> I put on righteousness (*tzadeqah*) as my clothing;
>> justice (*mishpat*) was my robe and my turban.
> I was eyes to the blind
>> and feet to the lame.
> I was a father to the needy;
>> I took up the case of the stranger.
> I broke the fangs of the wicked
>> and snatched the victims from their teeth. (Job 29:12–17)

There is one further word that encapsulates the Hebrew understanding of the world as God intended it to be and contributes to the beautiful mosaic of biblical justice. *Shalom.* This word is the word most often used throughout Scripture to describe God's intentions for the world. *Shalom* is used a total of 397 times in the Hebrew Bible. Its Greek counterpart, *eirene*, often translated as peace, is used eighty-nine times in the New Testament. Not only is the word abundant in the Scriptures, it is also translated into several English words. These include well, welfare, completeness, to make peace, at rest, at ease, secure, safe, to prosper, to be whole, and so the list goes on. You get the picture, it is an extensive and rich word. Wytsma defines it this way: "Shalom is the all-encompassing desire of God for peace and goodness throughout His creation."[38]

In Jer 29:7 the people were encouraged to work for the *shalom* of the city where they found themselves. This verse has been variously translated as seeking the welfare, working for the good, or seeking the peace of the city. *Shalom* is essentially public justice. It is an interest in how the political, economic and religious powers either enhance or hinder equity and justice to people.[39]

Philosopher Cornelius Plantinga says, "To be a responsible person is to do one's role in the building of shalom, the re-webbing of God, humanity,

---

38. Wytsma, *Pursuing Justice*, 25.

39. See Lev 26:3–13; Isa 32:15–17; Luke 10:1–12; Rom 14:13–20.

and all creation in justice, harmony, fulfillment and delight."[40] In the Scriptures, the *shalom* community was driven by the eschatological hope seen in Revelation 22. However, we also see that God's intentions for our world, as taught in both the Hebrew and New Testaments Scriptures, is a very concrete, realistic and perhaps even achievable vision. John Stackhouse goes so far as to say that *shalom* gets his vote for the best word ever! He explains it this way: "Shalom doesn't mean merely peace but flourishing, and in every respect, along every axis. Shalom means that each individual becomes an excellent version of itself; every relationship blossoms; every group realizes its potential; and the whole cosmos relates lovingly and creatively to God."[41]

Jesus built his theology around the concept of the kingdom of God. It seems quite clear in the Gospel accounts that what Jesus meant by the kingdom of God was simply the full living out of *shalom* upon the earth. The kingdom of God is *shalom* personified and particularized in the life of God's people.

Conclusion

Throughout this chapter, we have woven together six themes which build a missional theology for the people of God. This mission belongs to God alone and we are invited to respond to the call to be participants and collaborators in this *missio Dei*. Salvation is rich and broad and encompasses all of life and the cosmos in the now and the not yet. In the kingdom of God, we see a picture of the world as God intended it to be and this is the reason we are sent people. In the incarnation, we are offered a motif for how we are to engage with the world. As people created in the image of God we are given a responsibility to the world and also a lens through which we see others. Our missional theology is further enhanced when we consider the call to justice which is woven through God's rich intention for all of his creation, the flourishing of all things. The *shalom* of God lived out in answer to the prayer, "Thy kingdom come, Thy will be done on earth as it is in heaven." What a privilege to be part of that great purpose.

---

40. Plantinga, *Not the Way It's Supposed to Be*, 197.
41. Stackhouse, "Why Does God," lines 19–22.

Key Concepts:

Missio Dei: Mission belongs to God. Mission is God's sending heart, therefore not something the church does but rather something in which we are invited to participate.

Soteriology: The study of salvation. The full scope of salvation includes redemption for this world and the next, for individuals and communities, for the earth as well as humanity.

Kingdom of God: A sphere where God's rule is accepted in the lives of people. Where life is lived as God intended.

Incarnation: God embodied in flesh. Emmanuel, the "with us God." This offers a powerful motif for mission.

Imago Dei: Humanity is created in the image of God, which is a gift and a responsibility. It is also the lens through which we are called to see others as people of value and worth.

Shalom: God's desire for peace and wholeness of all people and creation. The context where flourishing is possible.

To Learn More:

- *The Mission of God's People: A Biblical Theology of the Church's Mission*, by Christopher Wright.
- *Kingdom Come: Why We Must Give Up Our Obsession with Fixing the Church and What We Should Do Instead*, by Reggie McNeal.
- *Incarnate: The Body of Christ in an Age of Disengagement*, by Michael Frost.

Moving On

We started this chapter by saying that when we talk about God we are engaged in theology. Christian theology is informed by the Scriptures so theology and biblical studies are interconnected endeavors. They are in conversation with each other. In the next chapter, we are going to explore further missional ideas with a specific focus on biblical texts. These texts shape us as the people of God. His story is woven into our story. So now we turn our attention to the biblical story of mission.

Chapter Two

Biblical Story

GROWING UP IN THE Salvation Army, you might assume I had exposure to a well-balanced smorgasbord of biblical texts and that these texts would form a strong foundation for mission. However, on reflection, my scriptural menu was somewhat limited.[1] It seems to have included a substantial main course of Matt 28:18–20 (the great commission) complimented by an entree size dish of Matt 25:31–46 (the sheep and the goats). It was clear, evangelism was the main course and should occupy our attention but a small side serving of practical service was acceptable, particularly if it was a precursor to the main course. Hardly a well-balanced diet! Beyond that I am not sure what broad sense of biblical mission foundations was ingrained in me.

When using just a few passages to understand the biblical story of mission we have to ask ourselves what have we missed. Or perhaps have we chosen to ignore some passages because they may make life awkward or force us to face uncomfortable realities. A main serving of evangelism with a side serving of service may appeal to our desire to just get out there and do it, but in the end, it short-circuits the depth and complexity of the biblical story of mission. Ultimately the most important question is what does the breadth of the Bible reveal to us about the heart of God? In this chapter I am not seeking to offer a survey of all the key missional texts or an in-depth technical study of key Scripture passages. Many good books have ably tackled that task and are worth consideration for further study.[2] Instead I invite you to learn how

---

1. Throughout this book we will use the words Bible and Scripture when referring to the Christian sacred writings.

2. See the end of the chapter for recommendations.

to trace the grand themes of God's story of mission as we read the biblical story together. Consider this chapter a sampler and a starting point to grasping the broad themes of mission flowing through the Bible.

Renowned missiologist David Bosch contends that "however important single, biblical texts may [seem to] be, the validity of mission should not be deduced from isolated sayings but from the thrust of the central message of Scripture. In other words, either mission—properly understood—lies at the heart of the biblical message or it is so peripheral to that message that we need not be overly concerned with it."[3] Is mission central for us? Is it worthy of our primary focus or should it simply be set aside in deference to more significant tasks?

Missional Hermeneutic

There are many ways that we can approach our reading of the Bible. Often, we approach it as a text about theology. We read with the analytical, systematic (sometimes dogmatic) eyes of a person trying to prove a point or build an argument. The reading of Scripture can be transformed when we bring new eyes to the task, eyes focused on mission. Eyes focused on the overarching story of God and the engagement of the Godhead with humanity and the created world. In reading it this way we encounter the heart of God. A heart focused upon a desire to restore humanity, and indeed all creation, into right relationship with each other and their creator. From the beginning to the end we can hear the heartbeat of a God of love who seeks to put things right. In that ongoing story we find the foundational themes, a biblical story of mission.

When I was a child I watched television one program and one focus at a time. Channel surfing was a chore because the closest thing to a remote control involved standing up and walking across the room to turn the dial. Today I switch freely across many channels, maybe watching several programs at once. I do this while simultaneously looking at my tablet device and mobile phone. Drawing themes together from multiple sources helps us grasp the bigger picture. Reading the biblical story with eyes attuned to mission opens us up to a larger reading of Scripture. This leads to a more thorough and meaningful understanding of mission. "A missionary hermeneutic of this kind would not simply be a study of the theme of mission in the biblical writings, but a way of reading the whole of Scripture with

3. Bosch, "Reflections," 177.

mission as its central interest and goal."[4] As I look at multiple individual stories my eyes are tuning into the grand narrative. Yes, the so-called great commission of Matt 28:18–20 is interesting and informative but I want to balance that with Genesis, Exodus, Isaiah, Luke, Acts, and Revelation: indeed, the whole of the biblical account. As people who seek to better understand mission, our first task is to seek to grasp the full extent of God's story—and the full extent of God's love for all creation.

As Christopher Wright puts it, "A missional hermeneutic proceeds from the assumption that the whole Bible renders to us the story of God's mission through God's people in their engagement with God's world for the sake of God's purpose for the whole of God's creation."[5] To read the Bible this way allows us to connect deeply with God's grand narrative. In the coming pages we will consider six passages of Scripture in order to introduce the broad themes of the biblical story of mission. Consider it an introduction, and an invitation to read the whole Bible with new eyes open to the missional themes of God's story.

Hebrew Scripture

It can be tempting to set aside the Hebrew Scriptures, or Old Testament, as largely irrelevant to our understanding of mission. As Protestant Evangelicals, we like to jump straight to Jesus and then move onto the story of the early church. Doing so shortchanges our full grasp of God's mission story. One easily overlooked passage that is actually crucial to our understanding of God's missional story is Gen 12:1–3.

"Go . . . and be a blessing" (Gen 12:1–3)

The Abrahamic covenant acts as a key turning point, not just in the book of Genesis but in the story of mission outlined in the entirety of Scripture. Genesis starts on a high note with the beautiful description of our creator God and his intimate relationship with all beings. However, things quickly deteriorate and chs. 3–11 outline a consistent theme of multiple mistakes by created humanity. "A central thread of the story of Genesis 3–11 is how God's historical purposes were misdirected by the rebellion of humankind. Human beings misuse their cultural power for selfish and exploitive

4. Bauckham, "Mission as Hermeneutic," 1.
5. Wright, "Truth with a Mission," 143–44.

purposes. They do not image the self-giving love of God in their rule of the creation and the creation of cultural and social life."[6] The pattern of human existence has established a clear path of disobedience. In Genesis 12 God begins to reveal the journey of redemption for all creation.

The Abrahamic covenant is a promise of blessing, but not one which is narrowly targeted. Abram is given a challenge accompanied by a blessing:

> Go from your country . . . to the land I will show you.
> I will make you into a great nation,
>> And I will bless you;
> I will make your name great
>> and you will be a blessing
> I will bless those who bless you,
>> and whoever curses you I will curse;
> and all peoples on earth
>> will be blessed through you. (Gen 12:1–3)

Go . . . and you will be blessed. Too often that is where we chose to stop with our reading and understanding of this covenant. A blessing upon one man, and as a result one people group, sometimes interpreted at the expense of all others. What comes next? Verse 2 ends with "and you will be a blessing" which v. 3 expands with "and all peoples on earth will be blessed through you." God's promise to bless Abram and his descendants was inseparably linked with a promise of blessing for all people groups.[7] Obedience and a radical new start are the requirements for Abram. If this pronouncement of blessing is to be realized it requires him to react to the guidance of God and depart from all he knew so that a new work can begin. A departure from what has been before into a new future is the challenge. Note also the communal dimensions of this covenant. The Hebrew Scriptures often speak in communal terms. Impact is to be experienced far beyond the individual and it has broad societal implications. In the wake of Abram, God seeks to act through the people of Israel as a community. This is a far cry from our inherently individualistic interpretations today. God

---

6. Goheen, *Introducing Christian Mission*, 105.

7. It should be noted that there is some scholarly debate regarding the Hebrew grammar in this blessing phrase. The *nif'al* is a passive stem which might be variously translated as a passive, reflexive or middle verb. For more read Dumbrell, *Covenant and Creation*, 70.

acts through community and society to bring a fresh start on a grand scale. The vision of God is so much broader than the individual.

Go and be blessed was not intended to be a self-centered election or a promise which elevated specific individuals into special relationship with God to the exclusion of all others. You are blessed, now be my agents of blessing. This broad recurring motif echoes down through the subsequent pages of the biblical story. So does the struggle that those who are chosen by God need to actually remember to be a blessing. A challenge the people of God often continue to struggle with to this day.

Michael Goheen in discussing this passage in his excellent book *Introducing Christian Mission Today* describes God's people as a "so-that people." We are "chosen and graciously blessed so that all might know God's merciful blessing."[8] The people of God are to be agents of blessing. The full dimensions of that blessing are yet to unfold, yet the intention is clear. God chooses to include the activity of people to bring about his mission of redemption. To be blessed is not an end point but a starting point. Privilege is not the end goal of being chosen. Rather, we are invited to be active partners with God in a mission so broad and wide that all will have the opportunity to connect with the blessing and redemption of God. This is not disconnected from the account of creation and subsequent failure in Genesis 1–11. Rather "God's intention to bless [Abraham], his seed and all peoples of the world is a reassertion of the original purpose for humankind."[9] This concept of blessed to be a blessing is so pivotal that we find it restated in varying forms five times in Genesis (12:3; 18:18; 22:18; 26:4; 28:14). In Gal 3:8 we read, "Scripture foresaw that God would justify the Gentiles by faith, and announced the gospel in advance to Abraham: 'All nations will be blessed through you.'" Paul refers back to this covenant as an announcement of God's intent for those of other people groups to also encounter faith. "It would be entirely appropriate and no bad thing, if we took *this* text [Gen 12:1–3] as 'the Great Commission.'... There could be worse ways of summing up what mission is supposed to be all about than 'Go . . . and be a blessing.'"[10]

8. Goheen, *Introducing Christian Mission*, 41.

9. Köstenberger and O'Brien, *Salvation to the Ends of the Earth*, 31.

10. Wright, *Mission of God*, 214.

God as Redeemer (Exod 13:17—14:31)

The people of God are called to be a blessing, but let us not be misled about who is the main mission activist in the Hebrew Scriptures. It is God. The story of the exodus is a defining story for the people of Israel and one that informs us about the origin and intent of mission. Exodus 6:6 says that God has seen the oppression under which they are suffering and that God will act to redeem them from their situation. Over and over their eventual redemption is ascribed to God (e.g., Exod 15:13). Unfailing love, leadership, strength, and guidance are characteristics of their God who redeems. The formative story (Exod 13:17—14:31) provides us with the first named act of redemption in the Scriptures and stands as an archetype for the redemptive work of God's mission. Central to the faith of the Israelites "is the firm conviction that God has saved the fathers and mothers from Egypt, led them through the desert and settled them in the land Canaan. They have only become a people because of God's intervention."[11] The great mission activist of the Hebrew Scriptures is God. God acts. God redeems. They are only continuing as a people because God has intervened on their behalf. God is their missionary redeemer.

The story of the exodus is a powerful one, but also a defining one for the people of Israel. As we trace the themes of God's story in Hebrew Scripture we see the redemption story being told and retold. God acting again and again to redeem. The Israelite identity is defined by relationship with a God who acts on their behalf and will redeem them, and the story goes on. "In the exodus God acted as redeemer and the event itself is called an act of redemption. In both respects (what it said about God and what redemption actually was for Israel), the exodus provides one of the key ways in which the New Testament interprets the achievement of the cross of Christ."[12] All God's people are invited to share in this understanding through the later redemptive actions of Jesus. The missional story goes on. The people of God have an identity defined by a God who acts to redeem them. God is our missionary redeemer.

One final point about the nature of the exodus narrative and its themes of mission. Often, we are tempted to offer a one-dimensional view of what redemption entails. At one extreme we will overly spiritualize and

---

11. Bosch, *Transforming Mission*, 17.
12. Wright, *Mission of God's People*, 97.

disconnect redemption from the realities of day-to-day existence, at another extreme redemption is purely an earthly act for our material benefit and lacks spiritual and supernatural value. So, what do we find in this first scriptural account of a redeeming God?

Christopher Wright offers this helpful summary:

> In the exodus God responded to *all* the dimensions of Israel's need. God's momentous act of redemption did not merely rescue Israel from political, economic and social oppression and then leave them to their own devices to worship whom they pleased. Nor did God merely offer them spiritual comfort of hope for some brighter future in a home beyond the sky while leaving their historical conditions unchanged. No, the exodus effected real change in the people's real historical situation and at the same time called them into a real new relationship with the living God. This was God's total response to Israel's total need.[13]

This is no one-dimensional redeemer who offers a limited salvation. The intent is far-reaching and carries political, economic, social and spiritual dimensions.[14] The mission heart of God responds on multiple levels to needs apparent within the created world. If we have been invited to join God as mission coworkers, blessed to be a blessing, then the same full-dimensional mission beckons our involvement. "*Exodus-shaped redemption demands exodus-shaped mission.* And that means that our commitment to mission must demonstrate the same broad totality of concern for human need that God demonstrated in what he did for Israel."[15]

Multidimensional mission weaves its way through the Hebrew Scriptures. The mission of God extends far beyond spiritual redemption. Justice is to be sought for those who are oppressed, foreigners are to be cared for, slaves are to be freed, and the physical world is to be used responsibly as an act of stewardship. The mission heart of our redeemer God is broad and practical in focus and those who have encountered redemption are invited to practice redemption in a way that impacts all aspects of their spiritual and physical existence.

There are many other important mission themes and sub-points we could trace through the Hebrew Scriptures but let us limit ourselves to one final passage.

---

13. Wright, *Mission of God*, 271.
14. Wright, *Mission of God's People*, 99–100.
15. Wright, *Mission of God*, 275.

Mission to All People (Isa 56:1–8)

Being blessed to be a blessing was an ongoing struggle for God's people. It is easier to focus upon being blessed. To focus on holiness which sets us apart and can at times tempt us into feelings of spiritual superiority. Through the prophets, God sent a variety of reminders to the people that they were called to bless all people. These appeals reach something of a high point in the scriptures sometimes referred to as Third Isaiah (Isa 55–66). Isaiah 56:1–8 offers a particularly poignant account as God indicates his inclusive intent of salvation for all.

These verses highlight two people groups who were considered outsiders and as such excluded from God's Temple: foreigners and castrated males.[16] Isaiah, however, indicates welcome and inclusion for them into the people of God. This narrative challenges the people of God to accept as insiders these people who were previously considered outsiders to the community. Outsiders, even those considered sexually suspect or ethnically and culturally impure, were extended a place of inclusion. This passage challenges the people of God to consider those they understood to be beyond the reach of redemption and to realize that God redefines even these as welcome.

If this challenge from God through the prophet was not confronting enough, v. 8 offers more revelation.

> The Sovereign Lord declares—
> > he who gathers the exiles of Israel:
> I will gather still others to them
> > besides those already gathered. (Isa 56:8)

Still others. Already two groups considered beyond the reach of God's redemptive work had been named as welcome. Yet the theme goes deeper. The boundaries have been uncomfortably stretched and extended in radical fashion but it appears God intends more. Groups without a name, perhaps groups yet to be discovered or understood. Still others can be gathered who previously could not be considered as recipients of the redeemer's work. God erases the boundaries of exclusion and proclaims a message of welcome to anyone. Even those excluded traditionally by religious categorization and legalism.

---

16. For an example of some of the laws specifically excluding these individuals see Deut 23:1–8.

God is the missionary. God will gather all people. The full extent of blessing to all nations is being unwrapped. God is prepared to act and extend inclusion to others even when his people will not. "The Lord himself is the missionary who gathers and rescues, not simply the dispersed of Israel, but also people from 'all nations,' in order that they may see his glory."[17] God is missionary and the universal extent of redemption is made clear.

New Testament

Reading the New Testament through a missional lens might feel more natural for some people than reading the Hebrew Bible this way. It could be argued that it is flawed to read it another way. The New Testament is largely written by missionaries. They wrote it as they faced the challenges of mission in new communities, with people from churches that they had planted. As J. Andrew Kirk puts it: "What a difference it would make to biblical studies if full justice were done to the Bible as a book about mission from beginning to end, written by missionaries for missionaries! Given its content and intent, how could one study it any other way?"[18] Let us again sample three passages to help us encounter the larger themes with our missional eyes. I started this chapter with reference to the Great Commission from Matthew 28. This is a key passage with important emphasis upon the verbal proclamation of the mission of Jesus. I do not wish to minimize it, but as it is so well known we are going to consider three other passages as we seek the broad mission themes of Scripture.

Holistic Mission Empowered by the Spirit (Luke 4:14–30)

Contemporary society is obsessed with mission statements. Luke 4 offers the closest Scripture can grant us to Jesus' personal mission statement, in which he quotes directly from Isaiah 61.[19] He reads,

---

17. Köstenberger and O'Brien, *Salvation to the Ends of the Earth*, 52.

18. Kirk, *What Is Mission?*, 20.

19. This text is from Third Isaiah. As previously discussed Isa 56–66 represents for many scholars the high mark in Hebrew Scripture for a sense of universal good news. From within this peak of Hebrew Bible inclusivity Jesus announces his mission.

The Spirit of the Lord is on me,

> because he has anointed me

> to proclaim good news to the poor.

He has sent me to proclaim freedom for the prisoners

> and recovery of sight for the blind,

to set the oppressed free,

> to proclaim the year of the Lord's favor. (Luke 4:18–19)

This "Nazareth manifesto" draws heavily on the Hebrew concept of Jubilee from Leviticus 25. By quoting it Jesus placed on his agenda both the broad inclusivity of Isaiah and the multidimensional mission implications of the Jubilee concepts.[20] Two aspects bear noting as we read Luke 4. First, the actual content of the Isaiah reading that Jesus claims as his own, and second the reaction of the listeners in Jesus' home town.

This manifesto in Luke 4:18–19 highlights both a sense of proclaimed mission where the good news is spoken, and also a deeply practical mission with strong implications for the poor, oppressed, and imprisoned. We can be tempted to spiritualize these concepts but given the Jubilee roots it seems that a socioeconomic dimension and justice focus is clearly part of Jesus intent. As Wright notes, "It certainly builds a holistic dimension into the mission that Jesus sets out for himself by reading this Scripture and claiming to be its embodiment."[21] Mission cannot only be a proclamation of spiritual news. Mission, in the understanding of Jesus, is also enacted on behalf of the oppressed and transforms lives in a physical way. Words are not enough. Eternal hope in heaven is not enough. Mission is a work of practical and spiritual transformation.

Furthermore, Jesus mission is Spirit empowered and Spirit driven. He does not stand in isolation either in the content of mission (continuing a mission God has already announced) or the equipping for mission (anointed by the Spirit). "Jesus is the Spirit-anointed prophet who announces the new era of salvation which he brings to pass as the anointed Messiah" (Isa 61:1–2; 58:6). [22]

---

20. Lev 25 outlines a radical plan for giving people a fresh start in the year of Jubilee (every fiftieth year) which was far-reaching and included the return of property, release of slaves and resting of the land.

21. Wright, *Mission of God*, 301. Wright quotes Hertig who asserts that Jesus radical mission based upon Jubilee presented a holistic mission in four aspects: proclaimed and enacted, spiritual and physical, for Israel and the nations, present and eschatological.

22. Köstenberger and O'Brien, *Salvation to the Ends of the Earth*, 116.

It is also worth considering the reaction of the crowd and the wider context of this encounter and their implications for mission. You might remember that in response to this sermon the crowd tried to kill Jesus. We can jump to conclusions and explain Jesus' near-death experience because prophets are often rejected in their own town. Yet we should note that according to v. 22, the initial reaction of Jesus' hometown was one of warmth and amazement. Tension rises when Jesus illustrates his point with two stories that speak of God's gracious work in the lives of people. The problem is the people in these stories were outsiders. Jesus makes it clear that the mission of God is not only to the Jews but also to the Gentiles. Again, we encounter a broad inclusivity in the mission of God which is confrontational and unwanted by those originally "blessed to be a blessing." The work of God is not constrained by cultural or national boundaries.

Alan Burns offers an anecdote about this text which might be of particular interest to Salvationists:

> The Methodist Church's Martyn Atkins once conducted an experiment with a group of around one hundred Salvation Army officers. He asked them to find in the Gospels a text that identifies the Salvation Army and distinguishes its unique mission. After some considerable discussion and debate, the officers agreed on Luke 4:18–19. . . . The strong social justice element in the announcement of Jesus as to his mission clearly resonates with Salvationists in the 21st century. This corporate passion has a strong scriptural foundation.[23]

Mission Without Borders (Acts 15)

It would be tempting to include Luke 24:46–49, or perhaps Acts 1:8 at this point because of the seemingly explicit instructions from Jesus to witness and expand impact out from Jerusalem and to the ends of the earth. In the first half of Acts we see the expansion of Christian mission in response to those commands. First, in Jerusalem and then expanding throughout Asia Minor and among the Gentiles. As a result, came a crucial occurrence in Acts 15 and it is this text which we will consider in more detail. It tells of an incident which was a determining factor in whether the mission of Jesus could be carried by his followers to the ends of the earth. Significant controversy about Jesus command was addressed by the Council at Jerusalem

23. Burns, *Founding Vision*, 65.

in Acts 15. It is important to note that the controversy is not focused on whether Gentiles should be included within the people of God. It appears that was already settled in the affirmative. Rather, the early church faced the issue of whether their expanding faith and mission should remain within Jewish cultural forms. Would this new faith be simply a sub-sect within a minor sect? Would it be hidden within Judaism and required to fully observe the Mosaic laws? Or would it move beyond social boundaries to become something broader and unbounded?

If the Jerusalem Council had ruled to keep Christianity as a Jewish sub-sect, cross-cultural mission could well have been stopped. However, with a letter stating "It seemed good to the Holy Spirit and to us not to burden you with anything beyond the following . . . " (Acts 15:28) the mission is given the potential to cross any borders. "At this point in the story, God's people must shed their single ethnic and cultural identity to become a community of many peoples, established in various places throughout the world, with a mission to every people and culture."[24] The mission of God now officially goes beyond any borders—geographic, cultural, sexual, or ethnic barriers are of no importance to God.

All Things New—the Kingdom of God (Rev 21)

In concluding our focus upon six scriptural passages highlighting the themes of God's mission story we find our way to the second last chapter in the Bible, Revelation 21. Historically this would not be among the most quoted passages for understanding mission, but in our attempt to grasp the grand picture of God's story it provides important concluding clarity.

In the Gospels of Matthew, Mark and Luke, Jesus speaks often of the kingdom of God, or kingdom of heaven. Jesus inaugurates the reign of God's kingdom and opens our eyes to the implications of living as participants of the kingdom of God—a concept we explored earlier in our chapter on the theological story. Living as part of the kingdom of God challenges us to have a focus far broader than simply the church. We are called to embrace the broad dimensions of mission for all people and all creation. The mission of God is not about building the church but living out the reign of the kingdom of God in society. Our lives announce this reign today in the way we live and act. The kingdom of God is here and now, but also in

24. Goheen, *Light to the Nations*, 151–52.

some dimensions it is still to come. Inaugurated but not fully realized. In Revelation we see a fulfilment of the kingdom in all its promise.

> Then I saw "a new heaven and a new earth," for the first heaven and the first earth had passed away, and there was no longer any sea. I saw the Holy City, the new Jerusalem, coming down out of heaven from God, prepared as a bride beautifully dressed for her husband. And I heard a loud voice from the throne saying, "Look! God's dwelling place is now among the people, and he will dwell with them. They will be his people, and God himself will be with them and be their God. He will wipe every tear from their eyes. There will be no more death or mourning or crying or pain, for the old order of things has passed away." (Rev 21:1–4)

Mission is not focused on final judgment and personal salvation. Too often we are inclined to personalize and spiritualize the mission end-point. I will be saved through the redemptive work of God as expressed through Jesus. Fade to black. The story is over. But that would mean ending our understanding of Scripture at Revelation 20 and neglecting the two final chapters that follow. However, "the Bible does not end with the day of judgement. Beyond the purging fire of judgement . . . lies the new heaven and new earth. . . . When we take our biblical theology of mission to the end of the line in this way, it generates biblical faith and hope—that irrepressible optimism that should characterize all Christian action in the world."[25] God makes all things new. Hope. Not just for personal salvation but for all creation. God makes *all* things new. A picture of the world as it should be. The kingdom of God fully come.

Again, we meet our redeemer. The God who liberates us from the situations that enslave. We see our part in a story which began long before we were born and will continue for eternity. Previously we have encountered the broad holistic concern of our redeemer for the physical realities of life, but note in this passage the hope-filled promise of a new heaven and a new earth. Holistic mission embraces an ecological dimension. This includes the redemption of all God's creation not simply humanity. The very final act of our mission story, our eschatological understanding, embraces far more than a redeemed humanity. It embraces a redeemed creation as well. A new heaven and a new earth. This is something that too often we overlook in our personalized and spiritualized versions of redemption. N. T. Wright warns us, "We need to be very clear about this, because so many pressures

---

25. Wright, *Mission of God's People*, 44.

are pushing the other way. *God made this world of space, time, and matter; he loves it, and he is going to renew it.*[26]

Mission makes all things new. Spiritual. Physical. The created world in all its diversity and stretching far beyond simply you and me. The kingdom of God on earth as it is in heaven. Our missionary redeemer God desires the renewal of all creation and so we too are summoned into that hope-filled journey of renewal. The created world is not to be obliterated but renewed. As partners with our mission hearted God we are reminded of the holistic focus of mission. This focus is not simply holistic for humanity but indeed the whole created order. Mission has ecological dimensions for our redeemer is the creator of Genesis 1 and the re-creator of Revelation 21. "The power of [Christ's] resurrection propels human history toward the end, under the banner 'Behold, I make all things new!' (Rev 21:5). Like its Lord, the church-in-mission must take sides, *for* life and against death, *for* justice and against oppression."[27]

Conclusion

> God's saving plan for the whole world forms a grand frame around the entire story of Scripture. His mission is bound up with his salvation which moves from creation to new creation. Its focus is on God's gracious movement to save a desperately needy world that is in rebellion against him and which stands under his righteous judgement. The Lord of the Scriptures is a missionary God who reaches out to the lost, and sends his servants, particularly his beloved Son, to achieve his gracious purposes of salvation.[28]

Through this exploration of the biblical story we have encountered a range of broad themes that are crucial to our understanding of the mission of God. Our God is a missionary redeemer who acts to bring about salvation. Not simply spiritual salvation but one with multiple dimensions: political, economic, social and spiritual. Those who encounter the mission of God are called to be coworkers, to partner in the work of holistic mission. We are blessed in order to share the blessing of God with others. The broad mission hearted love of God always has others in focus. While we

26. Wright, *Simply Good News*, 95.

27. Bosch, *Transforming Mission*, 436.

28. Köstenberger and O'Brien, *Salvation to the Ends of the Earth*, 263.

are often tempted to define who is an insider and who an outsider in the community of faith, God continually pushes the boundaries of inclusivity beyond religious and cultural barriers. Jesus announced his Spirit-empowered mission as one of word and deed, a redemptive mission proclaimed and enacted with broad social justice implications. Just as Jesus challenged the concept of who was inside and outside the community of God, the early church grappled with and then pursued a mission beyond cultural, sexual or geographic boundaries. Our missionary redeemer makes all things new, not simply a spiritual renewal for humanity but a physical renewal for the whole of creation.

At this point we will leave the big picture of Scripture, but let us take with us our new way of reading the Bible. Not as micro-passages or individual texts, but with eyes that are wide enough to tune in to the grand narrative of what our God of mission is doing. As we move through the next few chapters keep the grand story of our mission hearted God in view. Encounter the grand narrative again in the church's story, the story of The Salvation Army and in what we see emerging today around our world. As this chapter began I offered you the invitation to read the whole Bible with eyes open to the missional themes of God's story. Now the invitation broadens. Read theology, read history, read society with eyes always open to the mission of God.

Key Concepts:

Hermeneutic: The theory of interpretation, especially of biblical texts.

Missional Hermeneutic: Interpreting the Bible from a missional perspective.

Blessed to Bless: An interpretation of Gen 12:1–3. The people of God are promised that they will be blessed and simultaneously they are called to live as blessings to others and the world.

Redemption: The intervention of God who acts to save.

Inclusivity: The boundaries of exclusion are erased and message of welcome to anyone is proclaimed, even those traditionally excluded.

To Learn More:

- *The Drama of Scripture: Finding our place in the Biblical Story*, by Craig Bartholomew and Michael Goheen.
- *Recovering the Full Mission of God: A Biblical Perspective on Being, Doing and Telling*, by Dean Fleming.
- *The Mission of God: Unlocking the Bible's Grand Narrative*, by Christopher Wright.

Moving On

The theological and biblical stories have built a framework for Christian missional thinking. These are the ideas which shape the Christian message and its outworking in our world. You may have heard concepts like "timeless truths" or "unchanging beliefs." These terms can suggest that theology or biblical ideas are immutable. Yet, in reality, all biblical and theological thought is expressed in a lived context and is therefore adapted in time and space. We might say, God is Love, but how that is experienced and expressed in Edinburgh, Delhi or Toronto today will be shaped by the Scottish, Indian and Canadian contexts. What does love look like here and now? How do people experience God's love as good news today? No doubt, that will be vastly different to how it might have been experienced in Rome in 80 CE. The church has had to grapple with applying missional thinking and practice for over two thousand years. In the following chapter, we are going to explore how the church has done this. It is only a summary of the journey; however, it will help us to see how the ideas of the first two chapters were lived out throughout the church's history up until our own time.

CHAPTER THREE

Church's Story

Introduction

JESUS HANDED HIS MISSION over to his disciples in that great missional event we call the ascension. Since then his followers have certainly lived that mission out in very diverse ways. The story of the church impacts how we understand and express Christian mission today and is a vital part of our own story. In an attempt to better understand ourselves and our own concepts of mission it is important to briefly retell that story here. Of course, sketching the story of the mission of the church from apostolic age to the present day in one chapter is very ambitious. Not only due to the sweep of history covered by these years, but also by the myriad ways of interpreting those developments. However, despite the risks, we do so in the hope to glean something valuable from this story, albeit brief.

There are many approaches taken to this task of telling the story of the church. We could chart a geographical history of the church which would look something like this: Jerusalem to Rome, Rome to Europe, Europe to the world. A slightly broader approach than simply geographical would be to explore the movement and translation of the faith from one context to another, from Jewish roots to the Hellenistic-Roman context, from Barbarians to Europe and Empire and finally through to the shift of Christianity to the global South which we are seeing in our contemporary context. Bosch's seminal work *Transforming Mission* published in 1991 follows this path and suggests six epochs or paradigms of church history. These are:

1. The early church as recorded in the New Testament.

2. The Eastern Church in the period of the church fathers.

3. The medieval church taken as roughly 600–1500 CE.

4. The Reformation church in the sixteenth and seventeenth centuries.

5. The enlightenment paradigm, covering the eighteenth, nineteenth and most of the twentieth century.

6. The emerging ecumenical paradigm, developing at present.[1]

The survey which is to follow will sketch the church's story in three eras, pre-Christendom, Christendom and post-Christendom. In each section, we will consider some of the major developments and missional responses of the church. We will also share the story of someone who exemplifies an important aspect of mission in that era. It will of necessity be brief and attempt to paint only a broad picture of some key missional ideas and movements of the past two thousand years. We will outline some of the ways in which the church responded to the idea that "the gospel must be constantly forwarded to a new address because the recipient is repeatedly changing places of residence."[2]

Pre-Christendom

Contemporary believers might think that at the time of Pentecost, the Christian church was an entity of its own immediately separate to Judaism. However, it is clear that the parting of the ways was a gradual and complex process. Whenever we date this, it would be widely accepted that the destruction of Jerusalem in 70 CE was a seminal moment in both the dispersion and the formation of the early church. The early believers scattered to avoid persecution, but as history records, this diaspora also heralded a time of growth in the numbers and fervency of the Jesus followers. After Stephen was martyred the believers scattered and it is recorded in Acts 8:4 that they "preached the word wherever they went."

In these early centuries, it would seem that the attractive power and appeal of local congregations drew thousands to the faith. "We may take for granted that the mere existence and persistent activity of the individual Christian communities did more than anything else to bring about

1. Bosch, *Transforming Mission*, 185.
2. Thielicke, *How Modern Should Theology Be?*, 10.

the extension of the Christian religion. . . . These communities exerted a magnetic force on thousands, and this proved of extraordinary service to the Christian mission."[3] Many early church members lived countercultural lives. Christianity offered charity as well as hope, hospitality and solidarity, mercy, and equality.[4] "The early church broke down the barriers that has been erected in the Roman Empire between rich and poor, male and female, slave and free, Greek and Barbarian, creating a confounding 'sociological impossibility.' . . . The lives of the believing community, nursed and shaped by the biblical story, enabled them to live as resident aliens, as lights in a dark world."[5] This witness and the remarkable transformations of people from all walks of life were enormously attractive. In the context of the harsh reality of the Greco-Roman world, Christianity grew with new values, lifestyles and standards.

In fact, "the church cared so much about fellowship that the Jews and Gentiles converted to the faith broke down centuries-old barriers and ate at the same table."[6] This fellowship, which transcended barriers of race, sex, class, and education, was enormously attractive. The second-century apologist Tertullian explained something of the effective witness of these believers when he said, "We have the same kind of life as yours . . . without taking ourselves out of the forum and the marketplace, without renouncing the baths and the shops and the boutiques and the inns and all the other places of commerce, we live in this world with you" and this life was proving so attractive that he went on, perhaps with some hyperbole, to claim "we arrived only yesterday, and already we fill the earth."[7]

Of course, it is possible to romanticize this period and we should remember that there were very real failings of the church in this time. The universal fellowship which was so revolutionary has been no doubt idealized. Further, they capitulated to a particular strand of Greek thought thus incorporating a dualistic worldview into the church.[8] This dualism has been an ongoing obstacle and as a result holistic spirituality is still some-

---

3. Harnack, *Mission and Expansion of Christianity*, 434.

4. Stark, *Rise of Christianity*, 161.

5. Goheen, *Introducing Christian Mission*, 125.

6. Green, *Evangelism in the Early Church*, 180–81.

7. Sittser, *Water from a Deep Well*, 181.

8. Dualism was only one strand among many in Greek thought, however its impact in Christianity has been significant. See Tanas, *Passion of the Western Mind*, 130–37, for further explanation of Greek worldviews.

times illusive. Possibly the most notable failure of this time was the regrettable treatment of the Jews. Despite their flaws however, the early church demonstrated a magnetic appeal that drew thousands. Christianity grew exponentially even with the church being under persecution for much, if not all of that time. It is possible that by 313 CE there were fifty million Christians.[9]

Christendom

Constantinian Period: Major Themes and Missional Responses

The transition away from the early church period was ushered in by the conversion of Constantine in 312 CE. During a battle near Rome he saw a vision of the cross in the sky with an inscription that said, "Conquer by this," and he believed he was called to lead into battle with a likeness of that cross. His ensuing victory was credited to the Christian God and his later baptism made him the first Roman Emperor to embrace Christianity. The conversion of Constantine and following authorization of the church by the state was, by any definition, a red-letter day for Christianity. It subsequently became a dominant institution in society taking its place at the center of Western power and influence. The conflation of church and state brought with it a whole new set of opportunities, challenges and dilemmas. "The Constantinian church was now an established church enjoying political and cultural power. A new ecclesial and mission identity was inevitable."[10]

During this time, Christian celebrations and practices were given fresh legitimacy and cultural capital. These include the centrality of Sunday worship and the celebration of Easter, which were endorsed and sanctioned throughout the empire. There was a new freedom for Christians and resources were available for the church in mission. Historian Richard Tarnas lists some of the benefits that came to Western culture during the period of Christendom. They include ethical values, a high esteem of reason, the dignity and rights of humans, a sense of moral responsibility, care for the vulnerable and a future orientation.[11] In this period mission was often church-centered and the liturgy and Eucharist were salvific.

---

9. Jacobsen, *World's Christians*, 269.

10. Goheen, *Introducing Christian Mission*, 129.

11. Tarnas, *Passion of the Western Mind*, 169.

This era, despite many contributions to the Christian faith, has been heavily critiqued for its failings. There were the obvious corrupting influences of power and the growing damage done by political supremacy of the church in state affairs. Yancey has reflected that coziness between church and state is good for the state and bad for the church. This period was obviously the pinnacle of such coziness.[12] Another key development in this time was the emerging philosophical theology where "message became doctrine and doctrine became dogma."[13] Persecutions followed as a result. It is important to note however, as always: this time in church history was long and complex.

While the church was often powerful and influential an alternative missional response was the monastic movement. "When Christianity became the official religion of the Empire and persecutions ended, the monk succeeded the martyr as the expression of unqualified witness and protest again worldliness."[14]

A figure who exemplifies mission in this time was John Chrysostom, a church father from late fourth century. His name carries his epithet, Chrysostom means "golden-mouthed" in Greek and he is remembered for his eloquence as a preacher. He was a monk who later became a priest, where he gained increasing attention for denouncing the growing wealth of the church and the abuse of power of the ecclesial and political leaders. Chrysostom had an abiding concern for the poor and oppressed. While he was best known as a bishop and preacher, each of his sermons held moral and social lessons. His time as bishop was tempestuous and he finally died in exile, but not before challenging a church growing ever more wealthy and powerful each year.

Medieval: Major Themes and Missional Responses

The medieval period was a turbulent time, marked by invading armies and violent Crusades, plagues and public executions. It was ironically also a time of rich cultural exchange as crusading armies from England and continental Europe were exposed to exotic new art, architecture, and food from the Middle East and North Africa.

By the medieval era, the Christian Empire had expanded into Europe and the Eastern Orthodox and Western Catholic Churches had split. This

12. Yancey, *What's So Amazing about Grace*, 248.

13. Bosch, *Transforming Mission*, 200.

14. Ibid., 207.

split is known as the great schism and marks the time when the Eastern and Western churches separated in theology and structure. It is a division that still separates Roman Catholics and Protestants from the Eastern Orthodox Churches today.

As the church was dealing with the impact of the great schism, a new world religion was on the rise: Islam. The birth and rise of Islam proved to be the most momentous development of this period. Within a century of Mohammed's death, Islam had spread to Northern Africa, India, Spain, and even into France.

The rise of Islam ushered in a new period of missionary zeal within the church. We know their primary response as the Crusades. Mission in this period was largely seen as an institutional responsibility. The pope would initiate and commission mission, often through the means of missionary wars. Pope Gregory invoked Luke 14:23 to sanction the use of force to "compel" and "persuade" heretics and unbelievers to be brought into the church. During this period conversion was imposed by the state, not only in the use of force against individuals, but when rulers converted they would forcibly convert their subjects. This occurred in Norway, for example, which was violently Christianized in the late tenth century.

Imperial power and religious power were intertwined. This time is known for the brutal massacres of the twelfth and thirteenth-century Crusades to free the Holy Land from Muslims as well as in Central America as the Spanish Conquistadors forced conversion to Christianity. Neither the Crusades or the Inquisition could be considered Christianity's finest missional hour. The Crusades were influential; however, they could not be considered successful if success is measured as freeing the Holy Land from the "infidel" and reestablishing Christianity as the dominate religion in the region.

During this period, the monastic movement remained a positive witness in dark and violent times. "The significance of the monastic movement can . . . hardly be over-emphasized. Europe sank into chaos in about AD 450 and remained in turmoil for many years. Tribal incursion and migrations virtually destroyed the fabric of society. The most creative response of the Church to the challenge of the times took the form of monasticism. The disciplined and tireless life of the monks turned the tide of barbarism in Western Europe."[15]

Most medieval men and women thought that a properly organized society consisted of three estates. The nobility, the clergy and the commoner,

---

15. Bosch, *Witness to the World*, 112.

or, as Bishop Adalbero of Laon put it, "Here below, some pray, others fight, still others work."[16] One of the great men of this time who knew something of all of these three estates was St. Francis of Assisi. He was born into privilege and had been a soldier and imprisoned before visions from God led him to a new affinity with the poor. Francis began preaching and through his work founded more than one Catholic order, including the Order of Poor Clares for women. In a great transformation, St. Francis argued for the end of the conflict of the Crusades and embraced a simple faith. He advocated for the value and the place of the poor and also demonstrated a love of creation. His preaching to animals may be interpreted by some as evidence of mental instability, but has come to be celebrated as a forefather of contemporary Christian eco-theology.[17]

As the medieval period came to an end, another Italian, Christopher Columbus, was exploring new worlds under the auspices of the church. His voyage led to the first enduring European contact with the Americas in 1492. This ushered in a period of European exploration, conquest, and colonization that lasted for several centuries.

Protestant Reformation: Major Themes and Missional Responses

The years from 1500 to 1700 were yet again a time of religious, political, and cultural disruption. Catholic Europe was about to undergo a change which was to shape the imminent modern era. The next great schism in the church was at hand and it brought with it a new expression of Christianity and a fresh understanding of mission. Martin Luther became the catalyst for this major new paradigm which has come to be called the Protestant Reformation. Concepts such as salvation by grace, *sola Scriptura*, the priesthood of all believers, and the recognition of an individual's faculty for a relationship with God were central to the missional shifts at this time. The arrival of the printing press and the subsequent access to Scriptures for the masses were of vital importance to the dissemination of these new ideas.

The focus of this period was the renewal of the church. The mainstream reformers were focused on matters relating to local theology and politics. Subsequently missional responses beyond the local boundaries of the church were limited. Many reformers believed that the Great Commission from Matthew's gospel had been addressed to, and even completed

---

16. Janin, *Mercenaries in Medieval and Renaissance Europe*, 191.

17. E.g., see White, *Historical Roots of Our Ecological Crisis*.

by, the original apostles. The church in later ages had neither authority nor responsibility to send missionaries to the ends of the earth.[18] Calvin's theology of predestination with its suggestion that the sovereignty of God preceded and subsumed the responsibility of humankind also had the effect of diminishing missional zeal. Further, the reformers challenged the centrality of the church as mediator of faith and practice. As a result, a thorough individualism was encouraged. This echoes through the generations to us today.

During this period a group of believers emerged who offered an alternative missional narrative. These were the Anabaptists who were so named because they rejected infant baptism in favor of adults making their own informed decision.[19] Their beliefs, however, were broader than regarding baptism alone. They argued for the separation of church and state, that church should be simple, missionary, and pilgrim and that there was no need for complex ecclesial hierarchies. They also began to see Europe as a mission field and mission itself as the responsibility of individual believers rather than the pope.[20] The power of theological debate at this time is evidenced by the aggression and persecution shown towards the Anabaptists. This quiet evangelical movement centered on the common people and so there are not well known names from this group. Their missional ideas, however, were a great challenge to theology and the abuses of power during Christendom. These themes would play a significant part in the paradigm which was to come.

The End of Christendom

Enlightenment and Beyond: Major Themes and Missional Responses

The eighteenth century ushered in a new period of church history and mission, the Enlightenment. This was a time of revolutionary change within Western culture. Science, philosophy and politics heralded the shift from the medieval to modern worldview. During this time philosophy reached its height and there was a corresponding change in focus from god to

18. Neill, *History of Christian Missions*, 189.

19. The name Anabaptist means "one who baptizes again," however those holding this view rejected the legitimacy of infant baptism and therefore the name, claiming that adult baptism was in fact the first baptism.

20. Goheen, *Introducing Christian Mission*, 140.

humanity. Science birthed the industrial revolution and along with evolutionary theories led to optimism and a confidence in human progress.

One of the hallmarks of this period was the modern missionary movement. In tandem with the dominant Western culture, exploration, and colonialism, the church too saw huge expansion. When watching a video clip recently which charted the geographical growth of the church over the past two thousand years I was struck by how the first eighteen hundred years saw the church grow in a relatively small section of the globe. Then during the 1800s to the 1900s there was rapid expansion. This period has been characterized as mission from the "West to the rest".

William Carey is one of the best-known names of this era. He was convinced that the call of the great commission to make disciples of all people was still a Christian imperative. He responded personally to that call but also called others to join the missionary cause. Carey spent many years in India where he translated the Bible into various languages and where he advocated for the end to the Indian practice of sati, the burning of widows on husbands' funeral pyres. He is known as the father of the modern missionary movement and a social reformer. As with all people and periods of history however, he was a complex and nuanced character. While being remembered as the father of modern missions, some suggest that Carey was also a colonial ideologue who operated with thinly concealed prejudice.[21]

Florence Soper was another great character representative of this time. When she was in her late teens and visiting London, she passed a Salvation Army meeting in Whitechapel. She was converted and subsequently joined The Salvation Army. Her family was less than pleased that a respectable young lady was associating with the lower class and drunks, however young Florence was captivated by her faith and The Salvation Army. At the age of only twenty she was sent with Catherine Booth to commence the work of The Salvation Army in France. She left all that was familiar and secure behind her. It is not only noteworthy that a young woman would undertake such a daunting task, but also that the organization would invest such faith in two young women and send them virtually unaided to commence its operation in a new land. Upon her return to England she began to advocate for women in slavery. Her work was seen as instrumental in having the age of consent raised to sixteen. This made a significant reduction in intercontinental trafficking of girls. Florence married Bramwell Booth who was to become the second general of The Salvation Army and while well known

21. Pennington, *Was Hinduism Invented?*, 76–77.

for her role as his wife, is also remembered as a pioneering woman. She not only left security for the sake of the gospel at twenty years of age, but also started The Salvation Army's women's social work, a work which impacts lives across the globe to this day.

Other great names from this time include David Livingstone, J. Hudson Taylor, C. T. Studd and William and Catherine Booth. Mission was largely seen as foreign and it became closely linked with colonialization and the export of western culture. David Livingstone proudly asserted that "Christianity, commerce, and civilization had interests in common and could unashamedly support one another."[22] While this was a time of rapid geographical growth for the church, the gospel was, as Goheen says, taken to the rest of the world in Western dress.[23] What followed was often an appalling misuse of power and control which flowed from the mistaken belief that to Christianize was to Europeanize. Western dominance was assumed. Early missionaries conflated Christianity with westernization and were often unable to comprehend the one without the other. "Say what you will. Christian missionary work is frequently understood by the peoples of Africa and the East not as the sharing of an inestimable treasure, but as an unwanted imposition from without, inseparably associated with the programme of colonial powers."[24]

While colonialism was sometimes expressed through dress or practice, it was also expressed in the forceful and sometimes brutal domination of land and people. During this time, various European powers were penetrating and carving up these "newly discovered lands" for control. Jomo Kenyatta, the first president of Kenya, is widely attributed with saying that "when the missionaries arrived, the Africans had the land and the missionaries had the Bible. They taught how to pray with our eyes closed. When we opened them, they had the land and we had the Bible."

So, "like every era before, the modern missionary movement is marked by ambiguity. There is much to be grateful for and much that makes uncomfortable. There were both 'unspeakable horrors' and 'great achievements.'"[25] By the mid-twentieth century the great missionary endeavor was waning and colonialism was collapsing.

---

22 Walls, *Legacy of David Livingstone*, 126.

23. Goheen, *Introducing Christian Mission*, 145.

24. Neill, *History of Christian Missions*, 213.

25. Goheen, *Introducing Christian Mission*, 144.

A significant event which happened as this era was coming to an end was the 1910 World Missionary Conference, or the Edinburgh Missionary Conference. Many see this gathering as marking the inauguration of the modern protestant Christian ecumenical movement, or the genesis of the nineteenth century "movements of unity."[26] This conference championed ecumenism and unity, themes which have become major features of contemporary Christian discussion.

Post-Christendom

During the period of Christendom, the church held a place of influence and power in society. Much of the Western world was considered to be Christian. In the years since the Enlightenment, optimism has been chastened, the paramount place of reason is being challenged, and a more holistic view of the world is emerging. The central place and cultural hegemony of Christianity has waned in the West. We have moved into a period called post-Christendom. "Post-Christendom is the culture that emerges as the Christian faith loses coherence within a society that has been definitively shaped by the Christian story and as the institutions that have been developed to express Christian convictions decline in influence."[27]

Stuart Murray identifies some key transitional markers the church is facing in this move from Christendom to post-Christendom, keeping in mind that we are telling the story from a Western perspective and without the benefit of hindsight.[28]

- *From the center to margins*: in Christendom, the Christian story and the churches were central, but in post-Christendom these are marginal.

- *From majority to minority*: in Christendom Christians comprised the (often overwhelming) majority, but in post-Christendom we are a minority.

- *From settlers to sojourners*: in Christendom Christians felt at home in a culture shaped by their story, but in post-Christendom we are aliens, exiles and pilgrims in a culture where we no longer feel at home.

---

26. Hogg, *Ecumenical Foundations*, 31.

27. Murray, *Post-Christendom*, 19.

28. Chapter 5 will further explore the current trends in the Christian church today.

- *From privilege to plurality*: in Christendom Christians enjoyed many privileges, but in post-Christendom we are one community among many in a plural society.

- *From control to witness*: in Christendom churches could exert control over society, but in post-Christendom we exercise influence only through witnessing to our story and its implications.

- *From maintenance to mission*: in Christendom, the emphasis was on maintaining a supposedly Christian status quo, but in post-Christendom it is on mission within a contested environment.

- *From institution to movement*: in Christendom churches operated mainly in institutional mode, but in post-Christendom we must become again a Christian movement.[29]

Some who are reading this list may feel fear or even despair about this new paradigm. However, it may be helpful to consider that "far from foreclosing the possibilities for appropriate Christian living, these conditions actually open the door to new variations, new combinations of authentic and responsible action. The demise of Christendom reduces radically the temptations of power, clearing space for the old story to be retold."[30]

One of the great hallmarks of this era in the West is postmodernity. Much has been written about postmodernity. For our purposes, here we will identify a few distinguishing marks of this paradigm as it has shaped the post-Christendom West. One simple way to shed light on the shifts from modernity to postmodernity is to watch the opening sequences of two movie versions of Romeo and Juliet. First, watch Franc Zaffarelli's 1968 version, followed by Baz Luhrmann's 1996 version. These movies use exactly the same text from Shakespeare's great play, but they powerfully illustrate some key changes from modernity to postmodernity. In the Zaffarelli version a disembodied male voice dispassionately describes the scene from a distance. The scene is sequential and linear. Fast forward to 1996 and the opening scene is a celebration of the ethnic and the margins. A black woman appears through the static and heralds a frenetic scene into which the viewer is immersed. Religious iconography abounds. What we see here demonstrates four marks of postmodern culture, namely: fast / cutting and fragmentation, pick and mix lifestyle, tribalism, and the ethnic edge.[31] Post-

29. Murray, *Post-Christendom*, 20.

30. Lyon, *Jesus in Disneyland*, 147.

31. Taylor, *Out of Bounds Church*, 19–30.

modernity is also marked by the ascendancy of feeling and revolt against reason, the search for ever more sophisticated and expensive forms of pleasure, sports and popular artistic endeavor are experienced as religious celebration, the veneration of the body, materialism which elevates the place of consumption, and cynicism and bitter disillusionment in literature.[32]

Some years ago, John Drane explained why he always wrote postmodern with a hyphen. He said the hyphen represented something of the provisionality and evolving nature of the changes taking place and affecting our lives.[33] An increasing number of people are suggesting that the provisional period is coming to an end and we are entering a post-postmodern era.[34] Maybe the term postmodernity will be superseded. One suggestion gaining currency is that it will become known as late modernity and the new era may be called transmodernity. While postmodernity and post-Christendom overlap they are not the same phenomenon, however postmodernity has had a major influence in shaping our current era and therefore an important concept in this discussion.

Post-Christendom has seen the demise of dominance of the Western church. If the period of great missionary endeavor was characterized as Christianity from the West to the rest, then this period might be understood as the "Gospel from Everywhere to Everyone."[35] Goheen suggests that the church is present in every country in the world, its boundaries are equal with the inhabited world and this has led, for the first time in history, to a period of true ecumenism.[36] Bosch referred to this period as the emerging ecumenical paradigm. The changes in Christianity on the global scene will be explored in a later chapter. For now, it is important to mention that the decline of Christianity in the West and the growth of Christianity in the global South has seen the emergence of "World Christianity."[37]

Missional Responses in Post-Christendom

When Bosch was writing his seminal work in 1991 there was great hope for the missional impact of the ecumenical movement. The Second Vatican

32. Escobar, *New Global Mission*, 75–76.

33. Drane, *McDonalization of the Church*, 6.

34. Berger, *Day the World Changed*, 321.

35. Escobar, *New Global Mission*.

36. Goheen, *Introducing Christian Mission*, 152.

37. Walls, *From Christendom to World Christianity*, 306.

Council in 1961 promoted the cause of ecumenism. Ten years later the Lausanne Conference championed a global collaborative movement for missions with the stated vision of "the whole church taking the whole gospel to the whole world." In the intervening years, this great hope of Christian unity and ecumenical cooperation appears to be dimming. There are an estimated 40,000 different denominations in the world today. We may be left wondering how Jesus prayer for unity found in John 17 can be demonstrated in our time. The World Council of Churches' constitution is to seek "unity in order that the world may believe."[38] It would be fair to question how that unity is going in our partisan and increasingly adversarial culture.

There are those who still call the church to active collaboration and mutual respect. Sri Lankan Vitnoth Ramachandra believes that "a partnership that involves thoughtful, mutual listening among Christians from every tradition and culture within the worldwide church is indispensable for a faithful, united witness to Christ."[39] Sadly he is not optimistic that such partnerships or mutual listening will transpire but that does not stop him calling us to that ideal.

John Mott was an American who will be remembered for his ecumenical work and is considered by many to be the father of the World Council of Churches. He presided at the important World Missionary Conference in Edinburgh in 1910. He had an impressive commitment to international cooperation as exemplified by his service in 1916 as a member of the Mexican Commission, and in 1917 as a member of the Special Diplomatic Mission to Russia. During both world wars he worked for the relief of prisoners of war. He was also known for his criticism of the oppression of colonial peoples and challenged the church and society on issues of racism. In 1946, when he was the head of the YMCA, he was awarded the Nobel Peace Prize for his contribution to the creation of a peace-promoting religious brotherhood across national boundaries. Among his honorary awards are decorations from China, Czechoslovakia, Finland, France, Greece, Hungary, Italy, Japan, Jerusalem, Poland, Portugal, Siam, Sweden, and the United States.

Unity and ecumenism is one missional response of our time. Another is the exploration of spirituality. There are mixed messages regarding interest in spirituality in a post-Christendom West. It has been suggested that while the number of people attending church each Sunday was falling,

38. World Council of Churches, *Constitution and Rules*, line 14.
39. Ramachandra, *Gods That Fail*, 219.

spirituality in the West was on the rise.[40] David Tacey is one who argues that there is a significant emergence of contemporary spirituality. He speaks of an "upwelling of spiritual feeling in young people throughout the world."[41] John Drane agrees and suggests that there is ample evidence that people today are more open to the spiritual than they have been at any time in the past hundred years or more.[42] Findings like these give great hope to Christians who see this age of spirituality as an opening to sharing the Christian faith with a new generation.

It seems probable to me that the level of spirituality in the emerging generations may have been overstated. A study of the spirituality of young Australians today "did not find that Gen Y is a generation of spiritual seekers."[43] A UK study concluded that this generation do not demonstrate a God-shaped hole in their lives.[44] What is clear is that the emerging generations find their sense of meaning in the everyday. Social connection and relationships provide a key place to find such meaning. "The God of old-style religion is remote, detached, interventionist and supernatural. The God of the new spirituality, however, is intimate, intense and immanent. . . . God is not conceived as being extrinsic or outside super-reality, but as a mystery at the core of ordinary reality."[45] The spirituality of the emerging generation is grounded, incarnational and embodied. These themes connect deeply with a holistic approach to mission.

During Christendom salvation was primarily spiritual and future. As a result, evangelism and social action became torn apart as the concept of salvation was no longer big enough to hold them together. Dualism, imported by the early church from one strand of Greek thinking, influenced this limited view of salvation which held sway for much of Christendom. Today there is a move to unite the various aspects of future and temporal salvation through a more complete understanding of salvation. Social engagement, advocacy and social justice are increasingly understood as integral to Christian faith and practice.

40. There is more discussion on the fall in church attendance in the West in ch. 5.

41. Tacey, *Spirituality Revolution*, 2.

42. Drane, *What Is the New Age*, 202.

43. Mason, *Spirit of Generation Y*, 11.

44. Savage, *Making Sense of Generation Y*, 37.

45. Tacey, *Spirituality Revolution*, 163.

In some ways, it seems that current ideas about mission are modest, seeing it as a participation in what God is doing in the world. Some of the key contemporary missional tenets include:

Incarnational: For years, the church has sought to attract people and bring them into the church buildings. There is a strong imperative today to see ourselves as sent people. We are called to contextualize the gospel within our culture and context. While there is still a place of gathering, it is not the only or even the primary dimension of Christian life.

Narrative: Great truths of the faith are encapsulated in story. The church's elevation of systematic theology over narrative is seen by many as reductionist and life denying. Personal story and testimony are powerful in contemporary society which is often suspicious of propositional statements.

Holistic: We are integrated beings and God is intimately involved in the whole of life, and in fact all of creation. Dividing people or the universe into sacred and secular, body and soul, or temporal and spiritual are considered unhelpful and imaginary. People are integrated beings living in a fully integrated world and Christian faith is necessarily holistic in response.

Relational: Contemporary missional thinking values authentic relationships over organizational structures. Paid professional church leaders and complex hierarchies can be a barrier to missional engagement today. The priesthood of all believers and relational rather than autocratic leadership are key tenets of contemporary missional responses. "Emerging generations start out from a more psychologically resourced baseline than previous generations which brings with it an expectation of reciprocal relationships."[46]

Global, Diverse, and Inclusive: Contemporary missional conversations "cannot be truly attentive to the Spirit and to God's redemptive mission in the church and the world if it continues to ignore the voices and missiological perspectives of women, the marginal, the impoverished and the extraordinary missionary vitality and important theological voices of the Majority World contexts."[47]

As with every era preceding, the contemporary missional landscape is a mixed experience. There are places of deep connection of faith and culture and profound gospel engagements with the poor and marginalized. At the same time, there is rampant consumerism and other forms of syncretism, as well as decline in committed church attendance throughout the

---

46. Savage, *Making Sense of Generation Y*, 132.

47. Hill, *Salt, Light, and a City*, 271.

West. In a later chapter on the emerging global story we will pick up this narrative as we explore how the global church is developing today.

Conclusion

A popular television show at the moment is called *Who Do You Think You Are?* In the documentaries people are helped to trace their personal and family histories in order to better understand themselves today. This has become an increasingly popular pastime and genealogy and ancestry services are now big business. As people of faith we too look to our past to understand our present. Understanding our place in the great narrative of the people of God is important for our sense of identity and purpose. As we see ourselves within this great story of faith we will keep a broad vision but also be reminded of the part we have to play in writing our chapter of that story today.

Key Concepts:

Pre-Christendom: The period of early Christianity. Specifically, prior to the official endorsement of the Christian faith in the West in 313 CE.

Christendom: The period from 313 CE during which the church enjoyed a place of power and influence. During Christendom, much of the Western world considered itself both formally and officially Christian.

Post-Christendom: The current period during which the church no longer occupies this central place of social and cultural hegemony in Western civilization. Much of the West no longer considers itself to be formally or officially Christian.

To Learn More:

- *Introducing Christian Mission Today: Scripture, History, and Issues*, by Michael Goheen.
- *Post-Christendom: Church and Mission in a Strange New World*, by Stuart Murray.
- *Transforming Mission: Paradigm Shifts in Theology of Mission*, by David Bosch.

Moving On

Throughout this chapter, we have looked at the Christian church and how missional thinking has evolved and been applied in different eras over the last two millennia. The Salvation Army is a relatively recent development within the universal Christian church, being formed less than two hundred years ago. The Salvation Army is a particular interest to us and special focus to this part of the universal church is given in our next chapter. In particular, we will explore the story of The Salvation Army from a missional perspective. What is our part in the grand narrative of the church and how do we live out the mission of God in our contexts? It is to these questions we now turn our attention.

CHAPTER FOUR

Salvationist Story

YOU MIGHT THINK THAT a sensible place to begin exploring the Salvationist story is with William and Catherine Booth. That would be a lot like trying to describe my family story by starting with my parents. I carry a heritage. My grandparents and extended family have written parts of the story before me and I simply have the privilege to write the next installment. So, to begin this chapter on a Salvationist understanding of mission, let us briefly encounter the story of our "spiritual grandparents" in that of Wesley and the Methodists.

Wesley

William Booth once said:

> I worshipped everything that bore the name of Methodist. To me there was one God, and John Wesley was his prophet. I had devoured the story of his life. No human compositions seemed to me to be comparable to his writings, and to the hymns of his brother Charles, and all that was wanted, in my estimation, for the salvation of the world was the faithful carrying into practice of the letter and the spirit of his instructions.[1]

John Wesley (1703–1791) was an Anglican priest, passionate evangelist and social reformer who founded the Methodist movement. Catherine Mumford (later Booth) was born into a Wesleyan Methodist family. William encountered and joined a Wesleyan chapel in his youth. William's early

---

1. Green, *War on Two Fronts*, 10.

official ministry was within a variety of Methodist movements and even after their formal departure from Methodism in 1861 the influence of Wesleyan thinking over both the Booths and The Salvation Army remained strong.

While there are points of divergence between wider Wesleyan theology and The Salvation Army, there are several distinctive aspects of Wesley's theology, with its Arminian roots, which have impacted the Salvationist mission story. "In Wesley's theology, the atonement was viewed as unlimited and redemption as universal. . . . Wesleyan doctrine proclaimed a free salvation to whomever would believe, without the limits imposed by the doctrine of predestination. This made Wesleyanism uniquely adapted to world missionary thinking."[2] All people were worthy of the redeeming love of God. Indeed, all people were able to be reached by the Spirit of God, a strong contrast to the Calvinistic theology that dominated many expressions of Christianity both in Wesley's time and our own.[3]

Wesley held a view of humanity that affirmed that all are created in the image of God. As such all are worthy and possess the capacity to know God even though they have been impacted by sin. We can all be redeemed and restored into right relationship. This leads to something other than an inherently negative view of humanity. "This means the first word in evangelistic witness is not bad news but good news: Not, 'You are a sinner', but 'You bear God's image.' Evangelism starts with good news."[4]

In addition to the understanding that we are made in the image of God, Wesley held to the concept of preceding or prevenient grace, the gracious action of God that is already at work in all people seeking to draw them to God. "Prevenient grace affirms the universal salvific will of God, meaning that God wants everyone to be saved. . . . [God] continuously takes the initiative in extending grace to everyone everywhere, through the power of the Holy Spirit."[5] God seeks us out and there is nowhere we can go to hide from the grace of God. The missiological implications are rich; not only does God display strong intent that all people should be embraced by redemptive love, but also it affirms that God is actually the missionary and is active in seeking our redemption. We become partners, or participants in

2. Bennett, "Theological Foundations of Wesleyan Missiology," 68.

3. Here we will only consider two, but Snyder outlines five themes in Wesley's theology "that together constitute a dynamic theology of mission: image of God, prevenient (or preceding) grace, salvation as healing, the 'perfecting' of Christian character, and the restoration of all things." Snyder, "Missional Flavor," 63.

4. Snyder, Yes in Christ, 75.

5. Anderson, "Prevenient Grace in World Mission," 44.

God's mission. "The work of Christian mission is to cooperate with God's preceding grace so that people may experience God's convicting, justifying, and sanctifying grace."[6]

Wesley's theological convictions led him to a holistic expression of mission conveyed through social activism and reform. From his early days of ministry there was a concern for the poor and needy but we see a clear growth in the integration of the social and spiritual dimensions of mission as his life and ministry progressed. John Wesley influenced many to be involved in the movement to abolish slavery, most notably William Wilberforce. He was a strong advocate of the needs of the poor in general.

> What is remarkable about Wesley is that his commitment to social transformation is derived from his evangelical faith in the redemptive work of Christ and creation. He was able to see within the poor person covered with dirt and rags an immortal spirit capable of knowing God, loving him, and dwelling with him in eternity. . . . When he sees the poor, however degraded and disreputable, Wesley is convinced that he must show that person respect, honor, and love because that person is "the offspring of God."[7]

The work of Wesley and his Methodists was respected because people could see the positive actions in their lives. Words and deeds were consistent with the gospel message. This was not what many had experienced with the established church of the day.[8] Holiness, or perfect love, was displayed in love for God and love for neighbor and this would issue in practical actions to care for those in need. Wesley is famously quoted as saying "I look upon all the world as my parish." While at the time this was in defense of his right to preach in the open-air, it certainly reflected his missional conviction that all people, of all socioeconomic classes, of all nations, were worthy recipients of God's grace. Whosoever will may come!

"Wesleyan theology is saturated with hope, expectancy, optimism of grace and the grace of optimism. This hope is based not on human intelligence or technology but on Jesus' resurrection, God's promise, and the present work of the Spirit."[9] The Booths carried that hope and optimism with them into The Salvation Army.

6. Snyder, "Missional Flavor," 65.

7. Aboagye-Mensah, "World Our Parish," 58.

8. Hiatt, "John Wesley's Approach to Mission," 115.

9. Snyder, *Yes in Christ*, 27.

The Salvation Army

Sunday, July 2, 1865, is most commonly noted as the starting date of The Salvation Army (a name not adopted until 1878). On that date, William preached his first sermon in the East End of London in a large marquee on an old Quaker burial ground. His departure from the Methodist ministry was followed by years of itinerant preaching for both William and Catherine, although Catherine was more successful on the preaching circuit. An initial six-week commitment by William to revival preaching in the desolate, poor and spiritually neglected Mile End Waste became the beginnings of something far greater. Indeed, it is said that William returned home one night after preaching at Mile End Waste to declare to Catherine, "Darling, I have found my destiny." Surrounded by poverty, social evil, injustice, and people in need of redemption, the embryo of a work formed. This work was soon to be the Christian Mission, and later The Salvation Army.

Movement for the Poor

The poor and underclasses of society had held a special place in Wesley's heart and that same passion was evident within The Salvation Army. Perhaps it was William Booth's own experience of poverty as a child and what he witnessed in his apprenticeship to a pawnbroker that drove this priority. That may have been the origin, but what cemented this ministry focus was years of tough mission and ministry surrounded by the realities of poverty-driven heartbreak in London's East End. The poor were a growing priority, although it took some time for the Booths to seriously wrestle with the underlying social injustices that created the poverty they experienced. In its simplest sense, it was evident that the marginalized were just as in need of hope and redemption as anyone else, but most of society would shut the doors of their hearts, and their churches, to them. Where other doors were shut, this door would be open. Those excluded by most could find inclusion through the ministry of The Salvation Army.

The evangelical success of this mission to the poor is contested by some. Norman Murdoch in particular argues that the failure of Booth's East End evangelical mission led him to expand into other localities and priorities.[10] Even if there is some truth in Murdoch's claim, it seems evident that

10. Murdoch explores a range of early statistics to prove his point of evangelical failure in East London in his book *Origins of the Salvation Army*. He argues that evangelical

56

the needs of the community drove the mission of William Booth and the early Salvation Army. It was apparent that considerable growth of the early Salvation Army came from among working classes rather than the poor. Many of these working-class, and even upper-class individuals who came to The Salvation Army, discovered a passion to work with the marginalized. The story is told of William Booth in 1869 taking his eldest child, thirteen-year-old Bramwell, into one of East London's crowded pubs and saying, "These are the people I want you to live and labour for."[11] That challenge to young Bramwell continues as an ongoing challenge to all who consider their place in the mission of The Salvation Army.

It must also be understood that The Salvation Army stand with, and for, the poor was a radical one. This alignment with the poor made a significant difference to both individuals and to broader societal structures. Donald Dayton reminds us

> what a threat the Army posed to the dominant culture by its "turn to the poor." In one twelve-month period around 1880, 669 Salvationists were reported "knocked down, kicked, or brutally assaulted," 56 Army buildings were stormed, and 86 Salvationists imprisoned. We forget what a threat it was to conventional morality to have William Booth argue that prostitution was not caused by lack of virtue but was the product of such social forces as low wages that could not support young women flocking to London or to reject the double standard of sexual morality on profoundly feminist grounds. We forget that the mere movement toward the poor to identify with the poor is often so profound a move that it threatens the whole culture and appears to be "subversive." W. T. Stead in a biography described Catherine Booth as a "socialist and something more" because she was "in complete revolt against the existing order."[12]

The mission of The Salvation Army in full flight was not one to be ignored and the impact was palpable. To stand against power for the sake of the marginalized is a response worthy of those who seek to build the kingdom of God on earth as it is in heaven.

---

failure led to an emphasis on social reform to give the Salvation Army a credible future. We must ask was this failure or perhaps a discovery of a fuller sense of the biblical story of mission that opened new doors of redemptive possibilities.

11. Murdoch, *Origins of the Salvation Army*, 71.

12. Dayton, "Good News to the Poor," 88.

Adaptability and Innovation

One of the marks of mission success for the early Salvation Army was its ability to adapt and innovate. It seems that nothing was sacred and if a method could be adjusted or adopted in order to extend the mission then a new approach was welcomed. These approaches were not necessarily unique to The Salvation Army and other organizations tried some with limited success. However, Inglis attributed the success of the Army to the fact that, "with minor exceptions they were the only group of Christian evangelists of their time who approached working-class non-worshippers at their own cultural level."[13] Adaptation was a tool used to contextualize the mission and message of redemption. Early approaches ranged from using the common people's music, to adopting militaristic methods and uniforms in a culture that saw the military and colonial power in an incredibly positive light, to international methods such as truly living and working alongside the neediest indigenous populations in locations like India. God's message was not hostage to a particular culture or class and barriers were intentionally crossed. As Catherine Booth was reported to have said, "The Army's success has been built upon the great fundamental principle of adaptation."[14]

The number of alternate methods adopted by the early Salvation Army is almost staggering in breadth and variety. Equally, innovation could be quickly abandoned if results were no longer apparent. Space does not permit an examination within these pages but many initiatives are worth noting. These include the use of women preachers in a world were few women could aspire to work outside the home apart from prostitution or domestic servitude, the establishment of Australia's first motion picture company now considered the origin of the movie industry in Australia, William Booth's great motor mission of 1904–1905, the use of international travel and early telecommunications to increase a global mission impact, and the adaptation of modern management methods and structures. The early Salvation Army demonstrated a remarkable openness and preparedness to utilize the ideas and "tools of the world" to extend the work of God.

The dynamic impact of adaptability and innovation can be seen in the exceptional growth and expansion of the early movement. In the critical year 1878 when the new identity as "The Salvation Army" became fixed,

13. Inglis, *Churches and the Working Classes*, 187.
14. Cleary, *Boundless Salvation*, 46.

the movement was only to be found in Great Britain. It numbered some fifty corps with 127 officers. In the next ten years, the Army in Great Britain would grow to 1,445 corps and 4,314 officers but remarkably by that time its overseas work had expanded to 1,269 corps and 3,698 officers.[15] The first steps of overseas expansion had occurred in 1879 and by 1890 Army work was apparent in thirty-four countries. Clearly on a wider scale this was an age of mission expansion for Christianity. However, Murdoch notes that even in this context, by 1888 The Salvation Army was the world's fastest growing Christian sect.[16]

Overseas success was not necessarily consistent. The Army was more successful in countries under the cultural influence of the British Empire and most significant growth followed colonial patterns. While gaining a global reach, The Salvation Army remained culturally tied to England. Even today the colonial influence remains and The Salvation Army is largely at its strongest in former colonies of the British Empire.

Innovation and a progressive attitude gave The Salvation Army a remarkable mission edge that helped drive global expansion in its early decades. Philip Needham in his seminal work *Community in Mission* offers this cautionary note:

> The early Salvationist movement was positively brilliant and courageous at discarding forms which were irrelevant and adopting new ones that served the contemporary mission field well. But along with other denominations, it must today be willing to depart from many of the practices of its forbears in order to be faithful to what those forbears were doing in mission in their day—and most importantly, in order to be faithful to the God who *still* leads his Church in mission.[17]

Success leads to good reputation, reputation to respectability and respectability to a fear of innovation. It seems that the successful innovation of the early Army thus contributed to later mission inertia for the movement. Let us, however, hold that thought until the end of this chapter.

15. Read, *Catherine Booth*, 23.

16. Murdoch, *Origins of the Salvation Army*, 136.

17. Needham, *Community in Mission*, 58.

Holistic Mission

It can sometimes be tempting to speak about a person's theology, or theology of mission, as if it always existed in a static and fixed state. Reality is often very different. Our experience of mission, our engagement with the hurts and evils of the world, our discovery of grace and love in dark places help to nuance and refine our understanding of the person and work of God. Just as this appeared to have been the case for John Wesley it was certainly the case for William and Catherine Booth and the leaders of the early Salvation Army.

At risk of oversimplification it would be possible to describe the Booth's missional theology as having at least three stages which evolved over time. In the years leading up to the commencement of ministry in the East End of London they held to a fairly orthodox evangelical revivalist mission which was primarily concerned with personal spiritual salvation. During the 1870s a strong evangelical focus is still clearly the priority accompanied by a growing, but secondary, concern for the poor and marginalized. Several initiatives responding to the needs of the poor can be seen during this period but they were set aside when funds were short. Perhaps these responses to poverty were simply pragmatic reactions to evident need rather than the result of intentional theological reflection. However, an ongoing evolution of practice is evident. During the 1880s, and reaching some sense of maturity around 1890, there is clearly an evolving and growing sense of holistic mission. It balanced a concern for both spiritual and temporal, or earthly, salvation.[18]

This third stage represents the final development of the early Army's mission theology and offers our best understanding of a mature missional theology for the Booths. By 1890 both William and Catherine were in their early sixties with Catherine facing death from cancer before the year was out. Their shared experience in mission practice and understanding brought greater maturity. It is also arguable that the loss of Catherine may have impeded further change and ongoing evolution of missional theology as she had always been a strong and significant theological influence over William. "Catherine's soteriology was ethical and social to the core; salvation leads inexorably to the transformation of society and to the reign of peace and righteousness, the saving of individual souls is but the necessary

18. Green's work, *War on Two Fronts*, provides a thorough examination of the evolution of Booth's redemption theology and uses three categories dated pre-1878, 1878 until 1889–90, and from 1889–90.

beginning of the war in which the Army is engaged."[19] Catherine died a radical. She believed in the need and capacity for redemption to be enacted as both a spiritual and practical reality. Transformation now on earth, and for eternity.

The growing emphasis upon a mission comprised equally of evangelical, spiritual salvation and social activist, temporal salvation can be seen throughout the 1880s. Formal structured Salvation Army social work can be traced to a commencement in Melbourne, Australia. This was the Prison Gate Work led by Major James Barker in 1883 but other less organized approaches preceded this. The "Maiden Tribute" campaign in 1885 was a joint effort between the Army and others, most notably journalist W. T. Stead. It was designed to raise awareness of the sex trade in young girls. Stead and Rebecca Jarrett, an ex-brothel keeper who helped "purchase" a girl to prove the reality of the issue, were both sentenced to jail for their participation in this campaign. Bramwell Booth was acquitted for his involvement. Subsequently legislation was passed in the British Parliament to outlaw brothels and raise the age of sexual consent for girls to sixteen. In 1890 William Booth, assisted by others, including a seriously ill Catherine, wrote the book *In Darkest England and the Way Out*. This work represented a grand plan for temporal salvation and the establishment of new hope and possibilities for the poor on a grand and international scale. The vision was startling and while never fully realized, significant elements of the plan continue to find expression in Salvation Army mission to this day.

An article by William Booth entitled "Salvation for Both Worlds" and printed in 1890 explained it this way:

> I had two gospels of deliverance to preach—one for each world, or rather, one gospel which applied alike to both. I saw that when the Bible said, *"he that believeth shall be saved,"* it meant not only saved from the miseries of the future world but from the miseries of this also. That it came with the promise of salvation here and now; from hell and sin and vice and crime and idleness and extravagance, and consequently very largely from poverty and disease and the majority of kindred foes.[20]

This was not an abandonment of a focus on the necessity for spiritual salvation. Rather it was a growth in understanding of the fullness of the mission of the kingdom of God. The mission of The Salvation Army had

19. Read, *Catherine Booth*, 156.
20. Booth, "Salvation for Both Worlds," 2.

always been outward in its focus, never intended to simply be a spiritual club to care for the needs of those privileged to be on the inside. What emerged was a holistic sense of mission responding to the spiritual and physical needs of people.

There has been an ongoing struggle in the subsequent years to hold these two in balance as equal components of mission. Spiritual salvation and physical transformation need to be kept as a united and integrated whole rather than two divergent expressions of mission. Too often one is seen as a distraction to the other. Escott notes that "the period at which it [The Salvation Army] was most active politically (up to 1900), involving several campaigns . . . including the Darkest England programme itself, was also the time when it was most successful evangelistically."[21] A healthy marriage of the two was clearly possible but our tendency as a movement has been to enforce some kind of separation, or even divorce, within our mission practice.

Success Leads To . . .

A mission theology of The Salvation Army is grounded in a Wesleyan focus on God's preceding grace active for all people, a God who is active as missionary, and the belief that truly "whosoever will may come." This was enhanced by methodologies clearly focused upon the poor and marginalized, displaying adaptability and innovation. It was further marked by an integrated sense of holistic mission. One of the ironies is that these early missional achievements may have later contributed to the stagnation and decline of The Salvation Army.

A movement with a focus upon the poor and marginalized, or even the working classes, is often a victim of its own success. Ultimately a successful redemption focused mission will force a movement away from its roots making points of connection more difficult. Dayton calls this *embourgeoisement* where "a rigorous and highly disciplined ethical standard and the expectation of a radically transformed life under grace, bring a new discipline and focus to life that provides a form of upward social mobility that draws the movement more and more into the bourgeois middle classes and forms of church life."[22] This is sometimes referred to as "redemption and lift." A reformed and transformed individual makes a better home

21. Escott, *Church Growth Theories*, 329.
22. Dayton, "Good News to the Poor," 71.

for their family which opens doors of opportunity for their children un-heard of in their own generation. In many Salvation Army settings today, highly educated and upwardly mobile professionals tell stories of poverty and family dysfunction only two or three generations ago. The impact of spiritual and temporal salvation has literally transformed their lives. It has opened multiple doors of opportunity and advancement. Redemption is an ongoing practical reality. This comes at a price for The Salvation Army. One has to be intentional to achieve something that once came naturally. In many places, the distance to the poor and marginalized has grown and maintaining a connection now requires intentional effort. Success means we now need to nurture and encourage ways to retain our emphasis upon the marginalized.

The early years of the twentieth century saw what I would describe as a loss of confidence in our own theology of mission. This was coupled with an overconfidence in our methodology as a movement. The intersec-tion of these two proved a significant barrier. Goheen notes that "Between 1865 and 1930 a 'great reversal' took place in the Evangelical church that reduced the missional calling of the church to the verbal proclamation of the gospel."[23] These same years represent the peak period of expansion and growth for The Salvation Army. This was followed by the death of the founders, which arguably resulted in their original visionary initiatives be-coming entrenched as tradition.

The Salvation Army had been distinctly postmillennial in its escha-tology. It had a strong focus upon the transformation of the physical and spiritual world and a belief that The Salvation Army itself could help to bring about the kingdom of God on earth. This theology was positive and hope-filled, believing in the power of God to transform all things. However, the late nineteenth and early twentieth centuries saw a rise in premillenial-ist teaching based upon a particular literal reading of Revelation. It was a far more negative eschatology. This view held that Christians would be removed from this world before the judgment which would wreak destruc-tion upon humanity and physical creation. Salvationists were working to transform the world while other Christian movements were now choosing to view it as a lost cause.

At this time, there were also theological disagreements between evan-gelical fundamentalists and the Social Gospel movement who were often aligned with more liberal theological perspectives. The Salvation Army

23. Goheen, *Introducing Christian Mission*, 228.

was not in reality a part of the Social Gospel movement with our activist roots arising from our Wesleyan Holiness perspective, but the similarities marked us as suspect. These battles were largely won by the premillennial fundamentalists. Those dominant theological voices which offered a different heritage from Salvationist missional roots, contributed to doubt within The Salvation Army. Why did we have such a high view of humanity and believe the world could be transformed in multiple ways? Why did we do social work or social activism and was it really worth it? A profound mission theology of temporal salvation was in many ways transformed into simple obligation or good works that we continued to do, although we no longer really viewed it as "real" mission. Our missional success came to mark us as something less than true evangelicals.

The adaptations and innovations of the Army that had resulted in startling growth became enshrined as culture and permanent methodology. In many ways, The Salvation Army became its own empire, a world unto itself. We could proudly say that when you attended a meeting in Australia or Africa, the United States of America or South Asia you could feel at home and identify the forms and practices of worship as familiar, even the songs were the same. As we committed to maintenance of methodology and our own sense of cultural imperialism, we lost touch with communities in which we were placed to engage in mission. The capacity to contextualize the message was replaced with a need to enculturate new generations into the internal heritage of the Army. Adaptation was lost to stagnation. Innovation sacrificed at the altar of "this is how the Army does things." Our great success gave way to tradition.

Conclusion

Theological voices have moved on and the wider evangelical church has rediscovered the positivity of holistic mission and the fullness of the gospel. A new day is dawning for a hope-filled message of redemption for both worlds. A rediscovery of our own theology of mission can drive us into new effectiveness. Equally, the overconfidence in our enshrined methodology is coming undone. For many Salvationists in the Western world, it is now painfully obvious that holding to a traditional methodology has led to stagnation, ageing, and decline. A rediscovery of the fact that our true tradition is one of innovation and adaptability engenders hope for the future. "Evangelism and social action . . . are the twofold expression of a Church in love with the world for whom Jesus died and at war with every attitude, assumption, force and law which contradict the Kingdom."[24] Perhaps the new question is, do we love enough? As The Salvation Army are we in love with the world for whom Jesus died and will we recommit to our radical roots of mission impact? What is the story that you and I will write about the mission of The Salvation Army into the future?

Key Concepts:

Holistic mission: An integrated approach to mission in which all dimensions of life are valued. It includes the proclamation of word as well as the need for social action. It encompasses the present and the future, individuals and community, people, and all creation.

Wesleyanism: A theology shaped by the thinking of John Wesley. It includes key ideas such as a doctrine of salvation for whoever believes, prevenient grace, and holistic expressions of mission which includes spiritual and social concern.

Movement for the poor: A social and spiritual movement which holds a special place for the poor and underclasses of society.

To Learn More:

- *Community in Mission: A Salvationist Ecclesiology*, by Phil Needham (available as free download).

- *Yes in Christ: Wesleyan Reflections on Gospel, Mission, and Culture*, by Howard A. Snyder.

- *Blood and Fire: William and Catherine Booth and Their Salvation Army*, by Roy Hattersley.

Moving On

So far in this book we have explored missional thinking and practice through theological and biblical frameworks, and then through the lived

24. Needham, *Community in Mission*, 63.

experience of the church in general and The Salvation Army in particular. As the first section of this book comes to its final chapter we broaden our lens to look at what is happening across the Christian church today. This final story surveys how the global church is living out the mission of God today. In each part of the church and in each part of the world this is lived out differently. We will consider some of those themes and also consider some of the implications of this emerging global story for the practice of contemporary mission.

Chapter Five

Emerging Global Story

A recent UK headline read, "New Figures Reveal Massive Decline in Religious Affiliation."[1] Another from the United States says, "Why Nobody Wants to Go to Church Anymore," with the provocative byline that "the problem is worse than you think."[2] From Australia we read that "the proportion of Australians identifying Christianity as their religion has been declining over the last century—from 96% in 1911 to 61.1% in the 2011 census."[3] Similar stories could be told from most, if not all, Western countries. While these headlines grab our attention and maybe even sound dismal, they are far from telling the whole story of the trends in the contemporary church. The *Washington Post* offered an important counter point to the above alarming headlines when they posed the question "Think Christianity is dying? No, Christianity is shifting dramatically."[4]

The church is not dying. It is, however, changing. The center of gravity is rapidly moving. Christianity started in Jerusalem. Not long after which the center of gravity for Christianity moved to Constantinople (now Istanbul). For most of the centuries to follow it was solidly European or in European derived societies, and more recently North America. The story of the church we know has been Western. We had heroes like Luther of Germany, Booth of England, Billy Graham of the United States. On the walls of our Sunday school room was a painting of Jesus, looking curiously

1. Gledhill, "New Figures Reveal Massive Decline," line 1.
2. Schultz, *Why Nobody Wants to Go to Church Anymore.*
3. McCrindle, *Demographic Snapshot of Christianity*, 1.
4. Granberg-Michaelson, "Think Christianity Is Dying?," line 1.

Anglo-Saxon. Gathered around his feet were children from across the globe. We even sang that he loved all the children, red and yellow, black and white, but we thought he was like us, a Westerner with a loving heart to other nations of the world. Things have changed and Western society is clearly no longer the center of Christianity.

Recent years have seen a rapid and dramatic shift in where Christians are located in the world. Today the center of the church has been characterized as having moved from "Times Square in America to Timbuktu in Africa."[5] Philip Yancey explains the change this way: "As I travel, I have observed a pattern, a strange historical phenomenon of God 'moving' geographically from the Middle East to Europe to North America to the developing world. My theory is this: God goes where He's wanted."[6]

In 2002 Philip Jenkins wrote a book which was to become an award-winning best seller and heralded a new awareness of our contemporary Christian context. In *The Next Christendom* Jenkins tells us that the largest Christian communities in the world are to be found in Africa, Latin America and Asia. "If we want to visualize a 'typical' contemporary Christian, we should think of a woman living in a village in Nigeria or in a Brazilian *favela*. . . . By 2050, only about one-fifth of the world's three billion Christians will be non-Hispanic whites. Soon, the phrase, 'A White Christian' may sound like a curious oxymoron, as mildly surprising as 'a Swedish Buddhist.' Such people exist, but a slight eccentricity is implied."[7]

This change can be illustrated by the changes to administrative leadership within The Salvation Army. In 2009 the previously independent Belgium and French Salvation Army head offices were merged into one territory and in 2019 two Australian territories will merge to become a single territory. At a similar time, the growth in Kenya led them to divide into two, creating Kenya East and Kenya West territories. While there are many factors that lead to these decisions, on a surface level these changes reflect growth and decline of numbers within The Salvation Army.

While we could drown in statistics on a topic such as this, a few key numbers might help paint a picture of global Christianity today. There are about 2.3 billion professing Christians in the world, 1.6 billion Muslims, almost a billion Hindus and just under 0.5 billion Buddhists. In 1800, 23 percent of the world's population identified as Christian. Today that number

---

5. Ibid., 8.

6. Yancey, *God at Large*, 136.

7. Jenkins, *Next Christendom*, 2–3.

has risen to approximately 33 percent.[8] According to the International Bulletin for Missionary Research's recent report on religious statistics, Christianity is easily the world's largest religion.[9]

In 1910, 66 percent of all Christians in the world lived in Europe, today that percentage is more like 26. In 1910, 2 percent of the world's Christians lived in Africa, today it is closer to 25 percent.[10]

There is no doubt that the Western church no longer has the monopoly on Christianity. This shift to the global South will have enormous implications in the years ahead.[11] The church in the South is often found among the poor, many of whom face persecution. They are more likely to be ethically and theologically conservative and to have a stronger supernatural orientation. "The form of Christianity that has developed in the Southern Hemisphere and has reached the great Western cities is a 'popular' form of both Catholicism and Protestantism that we might well call 'grass-roots Christianity.' It is marked by a culture of poverty, an oral liturgy, narrative preaching, uninhibited emotionalism, maximum participation in prayer and worship, dreams and visions, faith healing, and an intense search for community and belonging."[12]

To help us understand the emerging global picture of Christianity, we are going to look at various regions across the globe and sketch a few key trends in each. A summary of each region will be followed by observations regarding the missional implications and issues of that region.

Africa

Christianity in Africa has grown rapidly in the past century. In 1920 Christians made up 10 percent of the African population but are now thought to be about 60 percent. About 400 million people in Africa identify as Christian.[13]

While growth has been experienced across the full expression of the church, it has been most notable in the Pentecostal and independent

---

8. Goheen, *Introducing Christian Mission*, 188.

9. Johnson, *Christianity 2015*, 29.

10. Johnson, *Atlas of Global Christianity*, 50–51.

11. As is the current convention Europe, North America and Australasia are referred to as the West, and Africa, Latin America and Asia as the South although these geographical distinctions are not at all exact.

12. Escobar, *New Global Mission*, 14–15.

13. Jacobsen, *World's Christians*, 163.

churches such as the African Independent Churches. This group is also known as African Indigenous Churches, African Initiated Churches, or just AIC's. They include churches from a variety of denominations. While the AIC churches are tremendously diverse, one thing they hold in common is that they were formed from African initiative rather than by foreign missionary endeavor. The use of traditional elements in worship and service are imperative. According to Thomas Oduro, the president of Good News Theological College and Seminary, Ghana, the AIC seek to establish *Afrikan ekklesia*, which are identified as:

> churches where the activities of the Holy Spirit are not constrained; where the liturgy is not regimented but vibrant and participatory; where the goodness and mercy of God are joyfully celebrated in diverse ways; where members are not inhibited but can express their exuberance in a language they can speak fluently and in a choreography that is common to the worshipers; where religious ingenuity is not stifled by bureaucracy; where the tenets of the Bible are upheld uncompromisingly; where the reality of demons and their activities is neither denied nor rationalized but counteracted; where sin and its effects are denounced unequivocally; where African spirituality is integrated with biblical spirituality; and where people are ushered into a wider Christian family—a family where pragmatic Christian care and empathy are emphasized and practiced.[14]

These vibrant and indigenous expressions of Christianity do attract some critique as being syncretistic due to the extent to which they have absorbed the paganism of traditional African religion. Of course, there is no cultural form of Christianity which does not take on the form of its host culture and so we should be cautious when making such a critique.[15] Contextualization of the gospel is necessary in every culture and a faithful African expression of the church has a lot to contribute to the world. That contribution will be felt keenly in the years ahead, not only as the African church grows, but also as African migration impacts western countries.

The Redeemed Christian Church of God is an example of this growth. This denomination commenced in Nigeria in 1952. Their goal is to plant churches within five minutes walking distance in every city and town of developing countries and within five minutes driving distance in every city and town of developed countries. While being an indigenous African

14. Oduro, *Arise*, 88.

15. Goheen, *Introducing Christian Mission Today*, 193.

church and active in seventeen African nations, they are also active in sixteen European nations, the United States, Canada, the Caribbean, Australia, Asia, India, Pakistan, and the Middle East.

Some of the issues facing the African church include the socioeconomic problems of African nations, the ongoing impact of colonialism and cultural imperialism, violence including profound Christian-Islamic conflict and the leadership crisis which come as a consequence of rapid growth.[16]

Latin America

The church in Latin America is also witnessing remarkable growth. It is has been estimated that "the Christian population in Latin America will grow to 640 million, or roughly the same as that of Africa."[17] It is comprised of two main groups, Roman Catholics and *Evangélicos*. Christianity came to Latin America during the sixteenth-century Spanish and Portuguese conquests. As a result, the population of Latin America is nominally Catholic. It is worth noting that while 75 percent claim to be Catholic, only 15 percent ever attend church.[18] While there has been some reform in the Catholic Church since Vatican II, it is the Protestant, and more specifically, the Pentecostal Church which is growing. Pentecostals account for 80 percent of church growth in Latin America.

Liberation theology was born in South America as a response to systemic and blatant injustice. The devastating poverty which grew from this injustice gave birth to this powerful force in Latin America. It is exemplified in the following story.

> A woman of forty, but who looked as old as seventy, went up to the priest after Mass and said sorrowfully: "Father, I went to communion without going to confession first". "How come, my daughter?" asked the priest. "Father," she replied, "I arrived rather late, after you had begun the offertory. For three days, I have had only water and nothing to eat; I'm dying of hunger. When I saw you handing out the hosts, those little pieces of white bread, I went to communion just out of hunger for that little bit of bread!" The priest's eyes filled with tears.[19]

16. Ibid., 194–96.

17. Granberg-Michaelson, *From Times Square*, 10.

18. Goheen, *Introducing Christian Mission Today*, 200.

19. Boff, *Introducing Liberation Theology*, 1.

In response to these realities Christians came to ask how to live out the gospel amidst such injustice. One response was that "there can be only one answer: we can be followers of Jesus and true Christians only by making common cause with the poor and working out the gospel of liberation."[20] Salvation in this context can only be understood as liberation from social, political and economic oppression. If the gospel does not address poverty it is not being true to its calling.

This crushing structural poverty has produced an ecclesiology informed by liberation theology. This is seen in the communal experience of a growing number of Christians who are rediscovering the meaning of the Christian faith for practical life. This ecclesiology is accredited with birth of the *comunidades eclesiales de base* (grassroots ecclesial communities or CEB). They have emerged as the new model for the church in several countries.[21] These communities are local grassroots expressions of church in the neighborhood or village.

The church in Latin America faces many challenges including poverty and injustice. However, the church's response to these issues has been complex and contradictory. Liberation theology and its expression within both established and CEB communities is often at odds with the prosperity teaching of the growing Pentecostal movement. Even within Catholicism itself there is much conflict. Furthermore, the monumental scale of the drug-trade in some countries is a huge challenge. Urbanization brings further complexity and challenge.

Asia

While much language of the growing church refers to the global South, it is also evident that the church is heading east as well. "Christianity grew at twice the overall population growth in Asia over the past century."[22] The situation in Asia is certainly uneven. The Philippines is the only country in Asia with a majority Christian population.[23] There are many places where the church is growing rapidly. South Korea has seen substantial expansion from 50,000 Christians in 1910 to more than twenty million today, growing from 1 percent to 29 percent of the population. Further, there is rapid

20. Ibid., 7.

21. Padilla, *New Ecclesiology in Latin America*, 156.

22. Granberg-Michaelson, *From Times Square*, 8.

23. Ibid., 9.

growth in Christianity in counties like "India, Nepal, Iran, Bangladesh, Cambodia, Vietnam, and, although unverifiable, North Korea."[24]

The growth of Christianity in China has received much attention, especially in light of the expulsion of Christian missionaries in the early 1950s. The restriction of Christianity and suppression of religious freedom did not diminish Christianity. Rather it saw the birth of Christian China. "Even though there was tremendous suffering and momentous persecution, what was left was Chinese Christianity, and Chinese Christians knew how to do the gospel in China without the missionaries. In a strange way, losing China was how the gospel took root in China."[25] At the time of the missionary exile from China there were thought to be about 4.5 million Christians in China. Today that number is a "statistical mystery" but possibly somewhere between twenty-five to two hundred million.[26] It is widely held that "the growth of the church in China has seen no parallels in history."[27]

Despite the remarkable growth of the church in China, it is important not to overstate the situation in Asia overall. The Christian population is still a relatively small percentage of those countries which have long and rich traditions in other major world religions. "The Muslim community has grown the fastest in that continent over the last century, with about one billion adherents comprising about one quarter of all Asians."[28] Furthermore many countries have political establishments that are hostile to Christianity. Finally, one of the great challenges of Asia is the urban challenge. Asia has seven of the world's ten largest cities and over two hundred mega cities.[29] These huge urban cities have enormous issues of poverty and social disadvantage with 60 percent of the population living in slums.

Middle East and North Africa

A quick survey of the church in the Middle East and North Africa is a salutary lesson for Christians from the West who cannot imagine a time when they do not dominate the global Christian story. This area was the cradle of Christianity and may well have once been considered entirely Christian.

24. Mandryk, *Operation World*, 59.

25. Jenkins, *Next Christendom*, 87.

26. Ibid., 88.

27. Mandryk, *Operation World*, 161.

28. Granberg-Michaelson, *From Times Square*, 9.

29. Goheen, *Introducing Christian Mission Today*, 199.

Today it is home to only 1 percent of the world's Christians. Half of the Christians in this region are to be found in Egypt and the situation is far from evenly spread. The dire situation in that area might be summed up in a recent article entitled "Suffocating the Faithful: Will the Last Middle East Church Leader Be Sure to Turn Off the Lights?"[30] After chronicling various atrocities committed in that region Jenkins concludes that "these experiences remind us of the sad historical lesson that persecution can indeed be very effective, if carried out with enough ruthlessness. Perhaps one cannot kill an idea, but it is not too hard to massacre or convert everyone who holds or expresses it."[31]

There is a great deal of diversity in how the state responds to Christians within the Middle East. Countries like Saudi Arabia and Iran are openly hostile and Christians are not able to practice their faith overtly. Other constitutions of many Gulf States affirm the freedom of religion to all but prohibit proselytization.

The Salvation Army commenced a ministry in Kuwait and Iraq through humanitarian aid. Later this work grew through the influence of Indian Salvationists working in the United Arab Emirates. Now there is a broader work in the Middle East Region. The Army, along with other churches, operates in UAE, Kuwait, Oman and Bahrain. The church is permitted in those countries as something of an unfamiliar necessity. They cater to the needs of a temporary population, the immigrant community who are already Christians. Proselytizing is not permitted. In the UAE The Salvation Army use facilities on a joint church compound and are required by law to hire guards to ensure no Emerati enter the services. The Christian church there is an immigrant church, with Indian, Filipino and English members.

Unlike other states, Kuwait has about 250 indigenous Christians who are Kuwaiti citizens. This small but growing indigenous church will face challenges as Christianity transitions from being a spiritual home for a majority of transient people into something more permanent and locally contextualized. While Saudi Arabia is officially 100 percent Muslim and Christians are not permitted to practice their faith openly, there is some evidence of a small but strong underground church in the area.

Diab says that in light of the history of the region it is vital today that Eastern and Western Christians work together, along with Muslims,

30. Aikman, *Suffocating the Faithful*, 58.
31. Jenkins, *Next Christendom*, 212.

to bring about reconciliation and peace.[32] This is particularly challenging with the rise of radical Islam in the region. Many believe it is unlikely that the church will grow or even maintain numbers in the near future, but Diab holds hope as "Christianity is, not only the religion of the Cross, but also the religion of resurrection."[33]

The Pacific

The Pacific region including Melanesia, Micronesia and Polynesia is home to about 34 million people, of whom 90 percent identify as Christian.[34]

As with so many colonized regions of the world, the development of a truly indigenous Christian church is a current challenge to the church in the Pacific. One current example is how colonial faith did not help the church deal with the issue of climate change. Pacific Island Christians are currently reexamining ancient beliefs which in the past supported an environmentally sound society and they are asking how an indigenous Christianity might speak to this issue.

The relationship between Christianity and nationhood is an important matter in this region. Unlike European cultures where Christianity has often been seen as linked to imperialism, Pacific Christianity has had closer links to the indigenous population than to the imperial powers. "The recent period in which the indigenous population emerged into national independence has revealed how closely the churches are tied to nationalism and the problems that result from these ties."[35] The result can be severe as it was in Fiji where ethnic prejudice against non-Christian minorities, legal privilege for Christians, and violence in the name of Christ transpired after the coup of 1987.[36] In contrast to these older, nationally oriented churches, denominations such as Pentecostalism and Mormonism are growing in the region.

32. Diab, *Middle Eastern Christianity*, 35.

33. Ibid., 54.

34. As previously explained, Australia is geographically part of the Pacific however because its Christian cultural landscape was inexorably shaped by European settlers and culture is considered part of the West in this discussion.

35. Forman, *Study of Pacific Island Christianity*, 103.

36. Goheen, *Introducing Mission Today*, 211.

Eastern Europe

Eastern Europe is the center of Orthodox Christianity and is also a region where the fate of the church is most strongly tied to that of the state. Goheen outlines three ways in which the church can relate to the state. They can be linked as they were in Christendom, the state can be hostile to the church or the state can be indifferent to the church. The church in Eastern Europe, he says, has faced all three in a century.[37]

In this region, Christianity is strongly tied to notions of national identity. The Orthodox Church even has a word to describe the ideal relationship of unity between church and state, *syphmonia*. While faith and nation can coexist, they can also be a toxic mix. This was seen in the ethnic cleansing in Yugoslavia and Serbia. In a previous chapter, we quoted Yancey when he said that coziness between church and state is good for the state and bad for the church.[38] We have seen that lived out in this region.

This is a region that is also still contending with the impact of communism upon the church. Decades of communist rule are bearing bitter fruit as churches deal with ideological influences and aspirations for state support with all its consequences. One of the challenges for this deeply nationalistic region is the engagement in ecumenical initiatives and inter-Christian dialogue. "Mission today is being done in a globalized world, and it cannot be purely 'Russian,' or 'Romanian,' or any other single cultural expression."[39] Kozhuharov is optimistic about Christian faith in this region. He says it is gaining spiritual strength and geographic expansion but future development will need to "keep the mission of the church as close to the mystical and liturgical roots of Christianity as possible."[40]

There appears to be a mixed assessment of the church in Eastern Europe today. Jacobsen says that "since 1990 the main story of Christianity in the twenty-one nations that make up Eastern Europe has been one of revival. After decades of Communist domination . . . the post-Communist era has been a time of religious recovery and advancement."[41] Jenkins, among others, would offer a more sober estimate of the situation.[42]

37. Ibid., 212.
38. Yancey, *What's So Amazing about Grace*, 248.
39. Kozhuharov, *Christian Mission in Eastern Europe*, 76.
40. Ibid.
41. Jacobsen, *World's Christians*, 88.
42. Jenkins, *Next Christendom*, 113.

The West

This chapter commenced with some dire headlines regarding the situation of the church in the West. It might be characterized as "thin but alive."[43] While Christianity is still a major force in the West, by any assessment the church is in rapid decline. The largest religious group in many Western countries is the "nones," or those claiming to have no religion at all.[44]

The Fresh Expressions movement in the UK grew from research in the Anglican and Presbyterian Churches. It concluded that "during the twentieth century Sunday school attendance dropped from 55 per cent to 4 per cent of children, meaning that even the rudiments of the Christian story and of Christian experience are lacking in most young people."[45] The Salvation Army in the UK is operating in similar context to where the *Mission Shaped Church* was written. It has also seen a major decline in the number of people becoming members. "Since the mid-twentieth century, the number of soldiers in the United Kingdom has fallen from 120,000 to somewhere around 38,000."[46] We could go on, but you get the idea. The church in the UK is symptomatic of the church in the West more broadly. "It took several centuries to convert Britain to Christianity but it has taken less than 40 years for the country to forsake it."[47]

Having said that, many people, even most people in some countries, still claim to be Christian. In Canada at the last census, 67 percent called themselves Christian. In Australia, it was 63 percent and in the UK, 59 percent. There is a great difference between those claiming Christianity and those who regularly attend church with the later a much smaller percentage in each country. The percentage of people attending church on an average Sunday in Great Britain is 10 percent, Denmark 4 percent, Australia 10 percent and France 13 percent.[48] In many ways the United States does not seem to be following the same trend as the rest of the Western church and Christianity appears stronger there. Those identifying as Christian and attending church is greater, however, as with the remainder of the West, the

---

43. Jacobsen, *World's Christians*, 132.
44. White, *Rise of the Nones*, 11.
45. Church of England, *Mission Shaped Church*, 11.
46. Yuill, *Leadership on the Axis of Change*, 14.
47. Brown, *Death of Christian Britain*, 1.
48. Kim, *Rise of the Global South*, 58.

church is still in decline. In 1980, 8 percent of American's claimed to have no religion. By 2008 that figure had almost doubled to 15 percent.[49]

Pentecostalism is a very important part of the contemporary Western story. This movement grew from the early twentieth-century revivals. "Their growth is spectacular—from virtually no Pentecostals in 1900 to over 177 million in 2010."[50] Another dynamic which is part of the story of the contemporary Western church is that of immigration. A professor of intercultural studies at RMIT University in Melbourne believes that the western suburbs of Sydney are very religious. "This is due entirely to immigration. Immigration is keeping the mainstream Christian congregations in the game as their older Anglo-Celtic and European followers die or drift away."[51] Immigration is changing the face of the global church, but possibly nowhere as markedly as in the West.

Issues and Implications of Global Trends

Having sketched a picture of the emerging global church, we wish to conclude by reflecting on some key issues and implications of these developments.

Migration

We have just mentioned the place of immigration in Western Christianity. Immigration is also playing a huge role in the global shifts of all major world religions. The movement of people across national borders is contributing substantially to contemporary shifts in global religious demographics. A French report suggests that Europe will admit seventy-five million immigrants by 2050 leading to what may be called "racially hybrid societies."[52]

While not all migration is from refugees, the impact of displaced persons cannot be overstated. At the time of writing this book Europe is facing the worst refugee crisis since the Second World War. The United Nations report that there are sixty million forcibly displaced persons around the world. The recent spike in those figures can be attributed to the brutal

---

49. White, *Rise of the Nones*, 13.

50. Mandryk, *Operation World*, 3.

51. West, "Leap of Faith for Church and State," lines 24–27.

52. Jenkins, *Next Christendom*, 121.

war in Syria.[53] Europe, North America, Australia and New Zealand are all recipients of large numbers of immigrants, many of whom come with a strong Christian experience. Granberg-Michaelson discusses the impact of immigration in the context of the United States. He says that much discussion of the impact of immigration is that often it is negative for Christianity. However, he contends that 60 percent of all migrants coming to the United States are Christians and are playing a role in reinvigorating churches, specifically the urban congregations.[54] Furthermore he holds out hope that Christian immigrants to the West will have a revitalizing impact. The multidirectional, cross-cultural missionary potential created by recent patterns of human migration is extraordinary. A key question will be how existing congregations, who have been shaped and molded by Western Christianity, respond to Christian immigrants. This "will be decisive for the future shape of Christian witness."[55]

Indigenous Expressions

Many of the growing churches across the globe are local expressions of Christianity. The gospel seed has been planted in local soil, and a local plant has grown up. People are increasingly hearing the gospel in their own language and culture. A Ghanaian scholar, Kwame Bediako says that the Christian faith is an "infinitely translatable cultural reality."[56] He claims African Christianity has overturned Western cultural dominance to become something truly indigenous.

Andrew Walls suggests that one of the ways in which Christianity differs to Islam or Buddhism is that historically, Islamic or Buddhist nations have tended to stay that way. Christianity, on the other hand, has been mobile and shifting. Unlike Mecca, previous centers of Christianity like Jerusalem, North Africa, Egypt, Serbia, Asia Minor or even Great Britain are no longer the center of faith. One of the reasons he suggests for this is that there is a certain vulnerability, a fragility, at the heart of Christianity, the vulnerability of the cross.[57] Another reason he offers is that no one owns Christianity. There is no Christian culture, but rather that the Christian faith is able to indigenize

53. Alfred, "What History Can Teach Us," lines 6–8.

54. Granberg-Michaelson, *From Times Square*, 81.

55. Ibid., 95.

56. Bediako, *Christianity in Africa*, 173.

57. Walls, *Missionary Movement*, 173.

itself in a variety of cultures. The incarnation stands as a central tenet of faith which leads to this wondrous gift of adaptation.

> The impossibility of separating an individual from his social relationship and thus from his society leads to one unvarying feature in Christian history: the desire to "indigenize," to live as a Christian and yet as a member of one's own society. . . . The fact, then, that "if any man is in Christ he is a new creation" does not mean that he starts or continues his life in a vacuum, or that his mind is a blank table. It has been formed by his own culture and history, and since God has accepted him as he is, his Christian mind will continue to be influenced by what was in it before. And this is as true for groups as for persons. All churches are culture churches—including our own.[58]

In the chapter on the church's story we explored how Christianity was often imported into cultures imperialistically and in western dress. The indigenizing of Christianity across the globe will be a powerful force in the years ahead.

Denominationalism

There are more than 45,000 different Christian denominations in the world today. In 1900 there were 1600 denominations. This is a 2712 percent increase in the division of the church in just over a century.[59] These figures make the very clear point that the church is, by any definition, ridiculously divided. Granberg-Michaelson's description of this situation is that Christianity is "endlessly denominated, geographically separated, spiritually bifurcated, institutionally insulated, and generationally isolated."[60]

Not only is there increasing diversity in denominations, but global denominations are starting to feeling the impact of the global South. Catholicism, the Anglican Communion, and The Salvation Army, among others, are already aware of the challenges of holding together an international organization in this context. The centers of power for these denominations have been in the West which is increasingly progressive. Yet the places the church is growing tend to be more conservative on issues of doctrine and morality. There is the further challenge of leadership which is just starting

58. Ibid., 7.
59. Johnson, *Christianity 2015*, 29.
60. Granberg-Michaelson, *From Times Square*, 27.

to flex its muscle. "Most of the world's ecclesiastical leaders are still based in Europe or hail from Europe. Catholics, Orthodox, Anglicans, Lutherans, Reformed Churches and many others still look to Europe for spiritual leadership. The Christian world remains profoundly influenced from Europe—ironic in that it is by far the most secular and least religious continent."[61]

Anglican scholar Radner has reflected on the cultural confrontations born of demographic changes within the Anglican Communion. He suggests that the theological and cultural tensions within the community have brought the communion to an existential crossroads. He predicts that the communion will not be able to hold together for much longer into the future. Recent struggles over sexuality are but expressions of this deeper theological divide.[62]

Granberg-Michaelson refers to this state of affairs as a "clash in worldviews shaped by Western and non-Western cultures, which influence the way in which the Bible is read, and faith is understood."[63] These global changes will require either genuine international power sharing or a dissemination of power and less centralized control. If not, the global communions will not be able to hold together. There will be interesting days ahead as we together seek to navigate what it is to be Christian, what is it to be a denomination, and what unity means in our time.

One final word on denominationalism. It is important to acknowledge the growth in Pentecostalism. While some might consider Pentecostals a recent or even exotic brand of Christianity, they make up over 25 percent of all Christians. They are a little less than 10 percent of the entire population of the world.[64] While being a very broad term, Pentecostals have a focus on the work of the Holy Spirit, including the supernatural demonstration of God's power and gifts as well as an exuberant worship style and a zeal for evangelism. Prosperity theology is common in Pentecostalism. These dynamics are not only attractive to countries in the global South, but are reaching a postmodern people of the West. Pentecostalism is growing against the overall trends in some Western countries. Some would go so far as to say that "Pentecostalism is the dominant force in global Christianity today."[65]

---

61. Mandryk, *Operation World*, 79.

62. Radner, *Anglicanism on Its Knees*, 46.

63. Granberg-Michaelson, *From Times Square*, 138.

64. Goheen, *Introducing Mission Today*, 180.

65. Kim, *Rise of the Global South*, 1.

Urbanization

The world is moving to cities. This both helps us understand some of the growth of Christianity and presents a challenge for the future. Tens of millions of people have left their settled rural communities and moved to cities. A recent UN report says that the world's urban population is expected to surpass six billion by 2045. Much of the expected urban growth will take place in countries of the developing regions. The largest urban growth will take place in India, China and Nigeria. In the past twenty-five years, the number of megacities with ten million inhabitants or more has grown from ten to twenty-eight. These mega cities are primarily in Asia and Latin America.[66]

Contemporary students of mission "will need to wrestle with urban issues if they are to be prepared for ministry in tomorrow's world."[67] Tomorrow has arrived. The world has moved to cities and the shift from rural to urban is every bit as profound as the shift from West to the South.

Tim Keller has reflected on what it will mean to undertake balanced ministry in cities. He suggests that meaningful urban engagement needs a variety of key elements including:

- Holistically serving the city, especially the poor, in word and deed.
- Producing cultural leaders who integrate faith and work in society.
- Welcoming, attracting, and engaging non-Christian people.
- Transforming character through deep community and small groups.
- Routinely multiplying itself into new churches with the same vision.[68]

Our challenge is to engage meaningfully in cities. To see them as rich places of mission and ministry and to partner with God. We might hear the challenge in the last verse of Jonah, saying to God's people, "if you love what God loves . . . you'll love the city."[69]

Conclusion

Some years ago, I saw an advertisement on television which showed a screaming woman being dragged from a car by a large man. It seemed

66. United Nations, *World Urbanization Prospects*.

67. Greenaway, *Cities*, xi.

68. Keller, *Our New Global Culture*, 13.

69. Goheen, *Introducing Mission*, 399.

obvious that there was some act of violence taking place against the woman and that the man was attacking her. Then the shot rewound and zoomed out. We watched the scene again, this time in wide angle. The new scene included the woman and the car which we could now see had been involved in an accident and a fire was seen not far away. The man who at first seemed to be a villain was now seen as a hero as he was rescuing the distressed woman who had been paralyzed by fear. The advertisement was for a television news show and the tagline was saying, be sure to get all the news, view it from the wider angle.

This chapter has sought that wider angle. It is important to take the broad sweep in order to see ourselves and our experience in context or we risk becoming myopic. We need to remember that countries and regions are far from homogeneous. The development of Christianity is uneven in each city and region, let alone country or continent. Such an overview requires condensing complex situations into broad generalizations. The development of Christianity across the globe is multifaceted and complex. However, we are global citizens and so understanding the Christian faith in an international context is more important than ever.

Key Concepts:

Global South: The nations of Africa, Asia and Central and Latin America.

The West: Nations including North America, Western Europe, Australia, New Zealand and some parts of Asia.

Indigenous Expressions: Expressions of Christianity which are shaped by local culture more than colonial power and influences.

To Learn More:

- *The Next Christendom: The Coming Global Christianity*, by Philip Jenkins.
- *The World's Christians: Who They Are, Where They Are, and How They Got There*, by Douglas Jacobsen.
- *The New Global Mission: The Gospel from Everywhere to Everyone*, by Samuel Escobar.

Moving On

We have called the first section of this book Thinking Mission. Our intention has been to tell stories which shape us as the missional people of God. Stories from Scripture and theological reflection, stories of the church throughout history and around the globe today and stories of one part of that church, The Salvation Army. These stories are foundational as they impact who we are and how we understand mission. However, the mission of God needs not only to be understood, it needs to be lived out. The second section of this book seeks to engage us in that endeavor. It is entitled Living Mission and each chapter explores a different dimension of how we live our mission as people of faith. We chose the word "Being" to head each chapter title in order to express that these issues were both dynamic and developing. Mission needs to be a dynamic lived reality for each of us. It is not a simply a way of thinking or talking. Living mission is a lifelong journey for both the church and for individuals. Let us take the stories that have shaped our thinking and see how these can be lived out in our practice.

SECTION TWO

Living Mission

CHAPTER SIX

Being Church

IN THE ORIGINAL *STAR Wars* film (now *Star Wars IV*) we meet a young Luke Skywalker who believed himself to be a simple farmer of no great significance. He was living an unspectacular life in an unimportant place and appeared resigned to his lot. On a daily basis, he faced hardships with the acceptance of many who lack the prospect of something more in life. Luke soon discovers a new life and a remarkable gift far beyond his imagining. As opportunity is thrust upon him he comes to understand himself in a new way. He gains a fresh appreciation of his own capacity and giftedness and as he finds his real purpose the lives of many others are transformed also. A life of meaning emerged as Luke came to understand his true purpose and potential. Self-awareness and self-understanding changed everything. In a similar way, a sound self-understanding for the church has the potential to radically alter our sense of purpose.

Ecclesiology

In the first section of this book we explored thinking missionally. Our second section has a focus upon how to live missionally. We start with missional ecclesiology, or to put it simply, what does it mean to be church. The study of ecclesiology is, at its core, a journey of self-awareness and self-understanding for the people of God, the church. Who are we? Why are we here? What are we to do? In ecclesiology, we explore the nature of the church and how we practice and express our life together. As we come to better understand what the church is then our sense of purpose and mission can take on greater meaning.

During Christendom, the church altered from being a mission movement to an institution. In this transition self-preservation and organizational life became central. The outward focus and the impulse to adapt diminished. Some may see this as maturation or simply a sociological inevitability. Whatever our preferred interpretation there was a marked change in what it meant to be church. This change placed mission as merely one of many functions of the church and often at the far edge of priorities. Guder says that "in the ecclesiocentric approach of Christendom, mission became only one of the many programs of the church. . . . Either we are defined by mission, or we reduce the scope of the gospel and the mandate of the church. Thus, our challenge today is to move from church with mission to missional church."[1] It is vital we reclaim mission as the heart of the church's purpose and practice.

Putting Order to Our Understanding

Alan Hirsch and Michael Frost offer one potential way of refocusing our ecclesiology. They argue that Christology must determine missiology, which then in turn should inform ecclesiology.[2] To put it simply, we must always start with Jesus and be defined by his priorities and sense of purpose. This will determine our own sense of mission as his people. Our Jesus-inspired mission focus will then inform us in the way that we structure and function as the church. Hirsch and Frost argue that for centuries Christology has been a priority but it was usually followed by ecclesiology. Mission often followed later as one aspect of the life of the church rather than its core. When we seek to define the shape of the church before we shape our mission, inevitably mission becomes lost, or at least minimized. Our identity and practices as the church must always emerge from mission and not vice versa. Christ shapes our mission and then our mission should shape the function and forms of the church. A focus on Christ and mission, before church, allows us to build a healthy ecclesiology. However, it is important to take an even broader focus and allow our understanding of the triune God to be our starting point for mission. It is the mission of "the Son and the Spirit through the Father that

1. Guder, *Missional Church*, 6.

2. This concept was explored initially in Frost and Hirsch, *Shaping of Things to Come*, and developed further in Hirsch, *Forgotten Ways*.

includes the church."[3] God is a sending God. The church is a sent people, an instrument of the mission of God's love.

As we read the Bible with a missional hermeneutic we encounter the inclusive mission heart of God. This transforms our understanding of what it means to be church. Church without a commitment to the *missio Dei* has tragically misplaced our priorities, or worse we have corrupted our true nature. The church can only ever truly be the church as it lives out the mission of God.

A correct self-understanding is important here. Just like Luke Skywalker, if we fail to see our true potential and purpose we can live unfulfilled lives that are limited in their impact for the kingdom of God. As the church, we need to understand why we are here: to partner with God in his mission. Everything else is subservient to that calling. Christopher Wright has put it this way: "It is not so much the case that God has a mission for his church in the world but that God has a church for his mission in the world. Mission was not made for the church; the church was made for mission—God's mission."[4]

Salvationist Missional Ecclesiology

The Salvation Army has had a curious journey with our ecclesiological self-understanding. We commenced as a mission movement rather than a denominational church and for many years staunch Salvationists resisted any efforts to refer to the movement as a church. There are still people who reject calling The Salvation Army a church. Yet the exercise was largely theoretical. We could deny the label "church" as much as we like but the sociological reality was evident: The Salvation Army had become a church. We hold much in common with many other denominations being influenced by their patterns, structures, and behaviors. The Handbook of Doctrine now includes a section on the Doctrine of the Church and in 2008 International Headquarters issued a publication stating that The Salvation Army is a denomination: a church within the universal church.[5]

On this ecclesiological journey The Salvation Army has adopted a more pastoral church model in which mission has been minimized to one aspect of our identity rather than being our central purpose. For

3. Bosch, *Transforming Mission*, 399.

4. Wright, *Mission of God*, 62.

5. Salvation Army, *Salvation Army in the Body of Christ*, 1

Salvationists mission is often seen as an additional program or activity. Pastoral care, Sunday worship, corps sections, music, welfare or advocacy, become all consuming. What is the place of *missio Dei* in the priorities of a Salvation Army Corps or center?

Contemporary Salvationists can integrate a solid understanding of our missional heritage into our current ecclesiology. Our missional ecclesiology connects us intimately with the very reason the church exists. We are called to partner with God in God's mission, we are sent ones. We are agents of the kingdom of God. We exist for mission and to understand ourselves in any other way is a misinterpretation of who we are.

This is not new. In the late 1980s Phil Needham penned what is now the classic theological exploration of ecclesiology for The Salvation Army. A good title always tells the story and Needham's work was titled *Community in Mission: A Salvationist Ecclesiology*. He says, "A Salvationist ecclesiology . . . holds that everything connected with the ordering of the Church's life and work must serve its missionary calling."[6] He called us to abandon any structure, process, ritual or program that impedes our participation and commitment to the mission of God.[7] The Salvation Army can only ever be truly The Salvation Army as it lives out the mission of God.

Understanding Our Purpose

What would the church look like if we measured every structure and activity according to their capacity contribute to the *missio Dei?* What if the kingdom of God was our measuring stick? Are we willing to set aside traditions and practices that are found wanting? What does a mission-shaped Salvation Army look like today? What does it mean for us to be a sent people?

Taking the time to understand and teach people of the grand and unfolding story of the mission of God is crucial. Talk about mission. Teach mission. Help people understand our mission heritage as Salvationists. Critically analyze current practices and address things that structurally stand in the way of the mission of God. Most of all embrace the missional heart of God. Join in the work of the kingdom of God around you every day.

Michael Goheen describes the church as "an alternative community for the sake of the world."[8] An outward focus is crucial for what it means to

6. Needham, *Community in Mission*, 57.

7. Ibid., 110.

8. Goheen, *Introducing Christian Mission*, 305.

be the church. We exist for the world around us, not for ourselves. The grand narrative of God's story pushes us outwards. We are motivated to see God's kingdom built here and now, in all its spiritual and earthly dimensions. A missional Salvation Army is always focused on others. We have a broad concern that all might encounter salvation in its fullest dimensions.

Mission Snapshot: Adelaide Congress Hall moved to the east end of the CBD twenty years ago. The Corps was between a pub and a strip club with a brothel across the road—the perfect place for the Salvos to be. While this was an urban setting, the Corps in many ways mimicked a large suburban Corps. Most of our congregation drove in to the city to attend church and did not live close by. For many years, we conducted a soup run to the homeless people in the city. A few years ago, we decided to hold the soup run on site each Saturday and invite people in for a sit-down meal. This ministry became known as DUO's—Do Unto Others. DUO's has grown and now serves 180 people each Saturday night. On Wednesday evenings, another 80 are served in an off-shoot ministry called DUO'S Express. Within a few months of commencing DUO's, a worship service started to follow the meal. The musicians for this service include regular Corps members and DUO's guests. People are always given the opportunity to share part of their story. Praying for one another is welcomed and frequent life transformations are the norm. The service is never a slick production, but the Spirit is always at work. One of the most beautiful outcomes of DUO's is the ownership that the established congregation has claimed on it. Many from our Sunday congregation volunteer to cook, serve, clean up, chat with guests, and lead worship. We are seeing evidence that the Sunday congregation, many of whom have attended Adelaide Congress Hall for many decades, are "being church" in the city rather than simply "attending church" in the city. *Matt and Clare Reeve, Adelaide, Australia.*

Being Attractive Is Not the Point

The Christendom church was marked by attractional approaches to mission. This was a belief that if only we run this program, or play the right music on a Sunday—then people will come and hear of God's love. Such methods and understandings still loom large in our imagination and are sometimes hard to break. No matter what we do in this new world we will not be attractive enough. Competition is too fierce and the world can entertain better and with far more glamour than we could ever hope to supply. Besides, being attractive is not the point.

As we learned in our earlier chapter on the theological story, Christ's mission was marked by incarnation. He moved into the neighborhood. Incarnation supplies us with a powerful image for mission. We are a sent people, not sitting in our buildings waiting for people to come to us. We join God in mission in our neighborhoods. We are invited to profound connection, to deep relationship, and to genuine engagement.

W. T. Stead, an English journalist, was jailed in 1885 for his part with The Salvation Army in the Maiden Tribute campaign against child prostitution. From prison, he wrote a series of letters and in one we find him grappling with what we would now term attractional church versus incarnational mission:

> Do you know what I think Jesus Christ would do if He came now? He would go to church and chapel ever so many times and listen, and no one would speak to Him. He would look to see who sat round Him and he would see no ragged people, no thieves, no harlots, only respectable people. And He would hear all these respectable people singing hymns to Christ, and giving all the glory to Christ, and then after standing it a long time, Jesus would stand up some day in the middle of the church and say just two words, "Damn Christ!" and then he would go out and go down some slum and put His arms round the neck of some poor lost orphan girl, who was having a bitter cry, and say, "Come unto Me, all ye that are weary and heavy laden, and I will give you rest."[9]

The Answers Are in the Margins

We may be tempted to seek a model or a program which tells us how to adopt a missional ecclesiology in our context. Five easy steps to being missional sounds enticing but is often ineffective. We fail to do the hard work ourselves to brings about genuine change. Throughout this book we are seeking to introduce you to a way of missional thinking to inspire new action rather than a set of easy steps. To be missional takes work and requires investment from us each.

One important place to gain inspiration is at the margins. If we seek out the creative missional edge of the church, including The Salvation Army,

9 Cleary, *Boundless Salvation*, 77.

we might be inspired and challenged by what we see emerging. Throughout this half of this book we offer some mission snapshots, telling stories of mission in local contexts. In addition to those be encouraged to look further and in places you haven't encountered before. As Leonard Sweet says in *SoulTsunami*, "The most creative places in nature, where life is born and renewed, are 'chaordic' zones. The most creative times in history are those hinge moments when chaos and order overlap."[10] Globally for several decades now we have encountered such chaordic times. We live in times of rapid and unpredictable change that we never could have imagined. It is also a time of incredible scientific advancement and technological order. Chaos and order come together to bring about creative new futures. The Salvation Army has better structures, access to technology, and systems than we have ever had before—order is something we do well. If we allow creative energy and chaordic ideas to birth new possibilities, the future is exciting indeed. Or are we fearful of how uncomfortable a creative new future may make us feel?

> The shape of the future is always on the fringe of normality during times of paradigm shifts. The changes are so immense and so encompassing that no one really knows where they are taking our planet in the twenty-first century. Only one thing is certain— nothing is normal. Who, then, do we turn to when looking for clues about ministry in the twenty-first century? We certainly cannot turn to those who insist on clinging to the status quo. We turn to the people on the fringe of normalcy.[11]

The status quo has reached its use by date. The current missional practice for The Salvation Army in the Western world has pockets of inspiration amidst a story of disconnection and possible death. What new stories of Salvation Army missional ecclesiology are being written today? Or perhaps more importantly what new story will we write?

Mission Snapshot: Hamilton Corps in New Zealand hosts a monthly worship event called the Gathering. This ministry grew from a desire for the corps and community ministries to work together. They started by considering which areas the corps and community services had in common. They concluded that the most overlap was in children's and family work. In response, The Gathering Saturday worship commenced.

10. Sweet, *SoulTsunami*, 81.

11. Easum, *Dancing with Dinosaurs*, 34.

The Gathering has a special focus on people who may not otherwise attend church. It is a reimagining of church. They seek to make a spiritual space where children and adults can come together. A typical night includes crafts, sports, teaching, singing, chatting, dinner, and more chatting. Each night, about ten activities are available. These range from crafts and woodwork, to relay races, sports and baking. Activities are of a high quality for adults as well as children. Each activity requires adult help, fostering a sense of purpose and belonging for both groups. A twenty-minute celebration time is the one aspect that bears some resemblance to traditional church and is always based on a theme. Recently one theme was "Winter Blues" where the activities included making hot-water bottle covers. In the celebration time we talked about how people deal with having the blues and that a great way to deal with anxiety is to talk to God about it. The evenings conclude with dinner. The concept is based on the Messy Church movement in the UK, which is about Christ-centered worship for all ages. This is worship which fosters creativity, hospitality and celebration. *Ingrid Barratt, New Zealand.*

Shaping Up for Mission

What are some practical steps for us, the church, to take to build our local shape for mission?

First, we need to see where God is at work in the neighborhood and discern how we can join in. If we are here for the sake of the community around us, we must be serious about understanding our neighbors and their needs. Get to know your community with its potential and its difficulties. What issues and unmet needs could be addressed and how can The Salvation Army bring God's love into that context? Ask questions. Meet and talk with community leaders: local politicians, heads of schools, police authorities, health and community service agencies. Taking time to sit in a local cafe, watching the community walk by and befriending the shop owners can bring many insights. Seek out the tools of government census and local government reports. Such research can reveal much about the local demographics but also the trends and issues that will emerge in the future. When God's Spirit places a point of clarity or a question in your mind, then chase down the information and see what God is calling you to do in response.

Second, build your team. Getting the team in shape for mission can often involve some cutting back as well as building up. Our local church can be a busy place with many priorities. Often the first step is to cut back the nonessentials so that we can fulfill God's mission. With that sacrifice of the old we can now start to equip people for what is to come. Training and encouraging people to get involved are crucial steps. Too often we assume people have the confidence or skills to join in with what God is calling us to do, but this may not be the case. Training is vital and will build confidence and the chance of effectiveness. Also, consider effective partnerships with other faith groups or community agencies. God is at work in the world and we don't have to try and achieve it alone. Building teams can stretch far beyond who is inside the walls of our building on a Sunday morning.

Third, share stories of success. In most places, only a certain percentage of people will join a new thing quickly so take the chance to tell the stories of what is happening. This will encourage wider involvement as people see what God is doing and begin to realize that they can be a part of mission as well. Stories change people's lives far more than statistics or cleverly written reports. So, let God speak through what he is doing in people as they join in the *missio Dei*.

Finally, think and plan creatively. Too often we look for the quick fix or predictable answers. God's mission deserves the commitment of your imagination and your planning skills. Don't limit the possibilities by sticking with easy answers. Continue to teach and talk about mission, and of course pray. In our prayer we seek the heart of God, we listen to the will of God and we become answers in the plans of God. So, pray, and then pray some more to see the kingdom of God here on earth as in heaven.

Sent Ones

Earlier in this book, and again in this chapter, we talked of the people of God as sent ones. This is in continuity with a Trinitarian understanding of the *missio Dei* and the incarnation. God the Father sends the Son, Father and Son send the Spirit. This movement is expanded into the world as the Trinity sends the church into the world as participants in God's mission.[12] We are a sent people and this is central to our understanding of the purpose of the church. This sentness can be connected with the concluding sequence of events in John's Gospel. In John 14:15–31 we hear the promised

---

12. Bosch, *Transforming Mission*, 399.

sending of the Holy Spirit as a comforter and teacher for the disciples after the departure of Jesus—God will send another to you. Later in John 20:21–22, following his death and resurrection, Jesus offers these words of commissioning for his disciples, "Peace be with you! As the Father has sent me, I am sending you." With that he breathed on them and said, "Receive the Holy Spirit."" We stand in continuity with the ongoing mission of God as sent ones. This is our identity. This is what it means to be church.

The arguments over ecclesiology are not yet settled. Within our part of the kingdom of God a conflict over identity persists. Kim Hammond and Darren Cronshaw in their book *Sentness* highlight the challenge:

> There are two competing postures for the people of God today: a church of consumers, demanding goods and services, and a church of missionaries, sent and sending into the world. These compete for the minds of Christians. Every church functions according to one or the other . . . two postures that shape all we do: selling or sending.[13]

Conclusion

We are invited to move forward with a firm self-understanding. We stand in continuity with the mission of God. We participate in the ongoing and unfolding story of mission. The church, including The Salvation Army, needs to live today as God's sent ones. We partner with God to bring about the kingdom of God on earth as in heaven.

To Learn More:

- *The Road to Missional*, by Michael Frost.
- *Mission Shaped Church: Church Planting and Fresh Expressions of Church in a Changing Context*, by the Church of England General.
- *Missional Renaissance: Changing the Scorecard for the Church*, by Reggie McNeal.

13. Hammond and Cronshaw, *Sentness*, 11.

Toolbox:

- matchfactory.org: This site is designed to support, resource and encourage Salvationists and friends in the business of justice-seeking and participating in political life.

- freshexpressions.org.uk.

- Search online in Verge Network for "Simple Ways to Be Missional."

- Search online for Community Needs Analysis for churches to find templates and ideas.

CHAPTER SEVEN

Being a Witness

I INVITE YOU TO think about the last time something truly wonderful happened in your life. Maybe it was an engagement, a new baby or a new adventure. Did you share about it? Why and how? Or maybe you can remember an exceptional new place you visited or a new device which revolutionized your home or work place. Did you share about it? Why and how? Sharing about something that brings us joy is a good place to start our thinking about witness and evangelism. It is the sharing of something positive and life-giving.

Sharing Something Good

"To evangelize means literally to offer good news or a welcome message"[1] and is an integral part of Christian mission. There are, however, many different ways of understanding what we mean when we use this term.

The World Council of Churches' 1975 statement on evangelism affirms that "the Christian community should be assisted to proclaim the gospel of Jesus Christ, by word and deed, to the whole world to the end that all may believe in him and be saved."[2] They go on to affirm the full scope of this claim by stating that "since our mission serves the coming reign of God, it is concerned with bringing the future into the present, serving the cause of God's reign, the New Creation. . . . We are called to exercise our mission in this context of human struggle, and challenged to keep the earth

1. Stone, *Evangelism after Christendom*, 9.
2. Adeney, *Graceful Evangelism*, 3.

alive, and to promote human dignity, since the living God is both creator of heaven and earth and protector of the cause of the widow, the orphan, the poor and the stranger."[3] This definition, along with that of most Christian denominations and organizations are what Adeney calls inclusive. They acknowledge that evangelism embraces both word and deed.

"We may, then, summarize evangelism as that dimension and activity of the church's mission which by word and deed . . . offers every person and community, everywhere, a valid opportunity to be directly challenged to a radical reorientation of their lives."[4] This is a reorientation around the triune God and his kingdom on earth as in heaven. Evangelism is nothing less than the proclamation of the kingdom of God and a gracious invitation to acknowledge that reality. Traditionally that invitation has often called people to a point of decision to follow Jesus. Through the work of James Fowler[5] and others it is further acknowledged that the journey of faith is also a process, with many points of decision along the way. Words like journey, process, development and pathways are often used to speak of the evangelism experience.

Metaphors for Being a Witness

Brian McLaren suggests we consider evangelism as conversation and not an argument, as making disciples rather than converts, and as a dance rather than competition. "The whole Christian message becomes for me less an outline of information and more a wonderful song. It is less a thesis to be argued and proved and more a mystery to celebrate and sing and dance."[6] In this conception, the sharing of faith is not about winning and losing but rather a genuine mutual sharing. A melody steals into our souls and we are caught up in the dance.[7]

Dance is but one metaphor, another might be that of the midwife. We are familiar with the image of spiritual birth, such as in 1 John 5:1 where we read that "everyone who believes that Jesus is the Christ is born of God." Following from this idea we might think of our role as that of midwife, a role which is not coercive but rather supportive to the bringing of new life.

3. Ibid.

4. Bosch, *Transforming Mission*, 430.

5. Fowler, *Stages of Faith*.

6. McLaren, *More Ready Than You Realize*, 150.

7. Ibid., 16.

A final metaphor is that of a gardener, borrowed from 1 Cor 3:6. We might prepare the soil and create the best possible context for growth. Or like Paul we might sow or like Apollos we might water, but it is God who brings the growth.

Within The Salvation Army, where the dominant metaphors are militaristic, we face a special challenge. If our guiding metaphors call us to conquest and victory, we risk using methods which are coercive or manipulative. We do well to heed the challenge that "Christian evangelism . . . is *pacifist* in every way. The good news is, as Isaiah said the good news of 'peace.' But this peace is not only the content and substance of evangelism but its very form. Christian evangelism refuses every violent means of converting others to that peace, whether that violence is cultural, military, political, spiritual, or intellectual. Evangelism requires only the peaceable simplicity of an offer and an invitation to 'come and see' (John 1:46)."[8] Isaiah celebrates the bringer of good news:

> How beautiful on the mountains
> > are the feet of the messenger
> who announces peace,
> > who brings good news
> > Who announces salvation,
> Who says to Zion,
> > Your God reigns! (Isa 52:7)

"But clearly today, evangelism does not always mean good news, and the feet of the evangelist are not considered so beautiful. For many people in our world, evangelism is neither wanted nor warranted."[9] Evangelism has been experienced by many, both Christians and non-Christians, as imperialistic and insensitive. Sadly, poor method and dogmatic content has meant evangelism is seen by many as an embarrassment to Christians and an affront to non-Christians.[10] Brian McLaren has characterized, and possibly caricatured how the gospel is often presented this way:

8. Stone, *Evangelism after Christendom*, 12.

9. Ibid., 9.

10. Ibid., 10.

information on how to go to heaven after you die . . .

with a large footnote about increasing
your personal happiness and success through God . . .

with a small footnote about character development . . .

with a smaller footnote about spiritual experience . . .

with a smaller footnote about social/global transformation.[11]

Sadly, I suspect we have all witnessed, if not practiced, such a limited version of the good news. In a previous chapter, we discussed how salvation has often been limited to something spiritual and future. It was often seen as individual and other worldly. As a result, much evangelism has been based on traditional notions of heaven and hell. The two alternatives are offered and people persuaded to take the heaven option before it's too late.[12] This narrow understanding of Christianity only as a "ticket to heaven" has diminished our faith and our lives. The focus of our Christian faith and therefore the manner in which we share it shapes both the message and the means.

Being a Witness to Good News

The gospel is good news and evangelism is the sharing of that good news. As we discussed earlier, it is alerting people to the reign of God in both words and deeds. We speak it and we do it. We say and we demonstrate the good news. Being a witness is something that we are, not merely words we say or actions we do. N. T. Wright suggests that mission must "urgently recover from its long-term schizophrenia. . . . The split between saving souls and do-ing good in the world is a product not of the Bible or the gospel, but of the cultural captivity of both within the Western world."[13] We must recover from this soteriological shrinkage[14] and recover a full expression of the gospel which embraces all life, people and planets, now and the future, spirit and body. Holistic evangelism sees the sharing of faith as a sharing of an inesti-mable treasure. God's kingdom has come, and we are sharing glimpses of it now while at the same time looking to the day when it is experienced in its

11. Frost, *Road to Missional*, 42.

12. Wright, *Surprised by Hope*, 226.

13. Ibid., 263.

14. See chapter 1 for more discussion on salvation and soteriological shrinkage.

fullest glory. Christ's followers are invited to create foretastes of that kingdom come. Pursue justice, love mercy, honor creation, work for *shalom*, live hospitably, include, embrace, reconcile, redeem and forgive.

> [Evangelism] will flourish best if the church is giving itself to works of justice (putting things to rights in the community) and works of beauty (highlighting the glory of creation and the glory yet to be revealed)—evangelism will always come as a surprise. You mean there is more? There is a new world and it has already begun, and it works by healing and forgiveness and new starts and fresh energy? Yes, answers the church; and it comes about as people worship the God in whose image they are made, as they follow the Lord who bore their sins and rose from the dead, as they are indwelt by his Spirit and thereby given new life, a new way of life, a new zest for life.[15]

Matthew 5:13–16 as rendered by the Message paraphrase offers us a way of seeing our role if we choose to follow Jesus:

> Let me tell you why you are here. You're here to be salt-seasoning that brings out the God-flavors of this earth. If you lose your saltiness, how will people taste godliness? You've lost your usefulness and will end up in the garbage. Here's another way to put it: You're here to be light, bringing out the God colors in the world. God is not a secret to be kept. We're going public with this, as public as a city on a hill. If I make you light-bearers, you don't think I'm going to hide you under a bucket, do you? I'm putting you on a light stand. Now that I've put you there on a hilltop, on a light stand—shine! Keep open house; be generous with your lives. By opening up to others, you'll prompt people to open up with God, this generous Father in heaven.

Mission Snapshot: When appointed as the Corps Officer at Gosford Corps I made a conscious decision to get involved in a community group so I joined a local running club. Sometime after joining the club I received a phone call from a Salvation Army officer at Territorial Headquarters which is opposite the city courts. A man from my running club had been in court that morning facing charges of fraud. After court Graham walked around the city for some time contemplating his life and how he had found himself in his present situation. Graham and I knew each other in passing and it was this connection which drew him to go to The Salvation Army. The person

---

15. Wright, *Surprised by Hope*, 203.

that was available at that moment was a gifted evangelist and shared about Christ and shared the gospel with Graham. He realized his need for Christ in that moment and became a Christian. Over the following months we shared often as he faced up to the criminal charges and began to make a change within his life. He started to live a life of integrity and honesty, he was a different man. Some months later Graham received a custodial sentence. At the time of writing Graham has been in prison for just over twelve months and in that time the transformation in his life has been astounding. He participates in weekly chapel and started a Bible study group. We write to each other regularly and Graham's letters are always full of faith, prayer and hope for the future. I joined the running club to intentionally place myself within the community. I wanted to use something that I enjoyed to make connections. Through this I met Graham. I am astounded at the transformation that I've seen in his life and am humbled to have been part of his journey. *Adam Couchman, Gosford, Australia.*

Absent or Empty Witness

There are two dangers which have become apparent in regard to evangelism. First, we sometimes see an almost complete retreat from any sharing of verbal good news. Good news is not spoken; the witness of a changed life may be partially visible but is not explained and given context as a life transformed by faith. People are attracted to the nature of our living but left perplexed as to its source and purpose. Alternately evangelism is sometimes practiced as totally removed from relationship. It is a disembodied transaction that ignores the communal nature of faith. Good news becomes something to be forced upon strangers rather than shared meaningfully in the context of ongoing respectful relationship. These both fail to grasp the beauty and depth of holistic evangelism.

Frost offers this perspective, "Part of the problem with evangelism is many Christians feel they need to get the whole Gospel out in one conversation. . . . Evangelising friends and neighbours, gradually, relationally over an extended time, means the breadth and beauty of the gospel can be expressed slowly without the urgency of the one-off pitch. When we understand what it is to be truly missional—incarnated deeply within a local host community—we will find that evangelism is best done slowly, deliberately, in the context of a loving community."[16] The verbal sharing of good news occurs best within a meaningful context of relationship. This is not to say that a faith conversation with a stranger could never occur, but rather that ongoing engagement over time offers grace-filled opportunity for genuine transformation by the good news. This understanding of the need to ground our verbal witness in meaningful relationship brings us to a key context for meaningful evangelistic encounter.

Hospitality and Welcome

Welcome and hospitality are central to a holistic understanding of evangelism and in this regard Jesus modelled for us a way of living. He was known for welcoming sinners and eating with them (Luke 15:2). Welcome and hospitality are not optional extras: they are both message and means. Welcome is the message of the kingdom. Hospitality is the demonstration of that welcome. How we offer hospitality says a lot about us. When we express it in response to our faith we are making a theological statement. When we extend welcome and hospitality to those who would not normally be in our orbit, we communicate expansive and inclusive love. I am not talking about the sort of hospitality requiring a hostess with the mostest laying a spread of food worthy of a reality television cooking show. True hospitality is a way of life which offers welcome to others. It involves treating strangers as equals and creating space for all to flourish.

The Scriptures offer hospitality as a core value for believers. In the Hebrew Bible, we read that Israel was to live out welcome in their dealings with others. "He defends the cause of the fatherless and the widow, and loves the foreigner residing among you, giving them food and clothing. And you are to love those who are foreigners, for you yourselves were foreigners in Egypt" (Deut 10:18–19). The gospels pick up the refrain: "But when you give a banquet, invite the poor, the crippled, the lame, the blind" (Luke 14:13). And the letters continue the theme: "Do not forget to show hospitality to strangers, for by so doing some people have shown hospitality to angels without knowing it" (Heb 13:2).

There are over one hundred references to food and drink in Luke and Acts and these books enhance how we understand our calling to witness through hospitality. There is a care for body and soul here. Our daily bread is not just spiritual, it is material and the gospel must be a call to good

16. Frost, *Road to Missional*, 44.

news for all areas of life. Food is presented as a symbol of the inclusiveness of the gospel. Jesus calls a people who had strict dietary standards to "eat whatever is set before you" (Luke 10:8). In this instruction, we hear a call towards inclusiveness and relationships. The sharing of meals and practice of hospitality become places of belonging and of genuine encounter, with each other and with God. We see this on the Emmaus Road, in the home of Simon the Pharisee and Zacchaeus the tax collector and in the breaking of bread before and after the resurrection. Intentional hospitality connects people and says, the grace of God welcomes all. There is room at the table for everyone. I have often wondered if some of the power of the evangelistic Alpha course is in the simple decision to base it around a meal table.

The whole sweep of Scripture offers a theme of hospitality as key to how God works through individuals and communities. While in "conventional hospitality people welcome family, friends and influential acquaintances, Christian hospitality ought to focus on welcoming the vulnerable and the poor into one's homes and community of faith . . . such hospitality would reflect God's greater hospitality that welcomes the undeserving, provides for lonely with a home, and sets a banquet table for the hungry."[17]

Christian hospitality does not flow in one direction alone. When we genuinely encounter others, and are open to those different to ourselves, we are changed. If you are old enough, you might remember the Christian song from the 1970s called the Servant Song. I think there is great insight in the final line that asks that we might have the grace to be served as well as serve. Our encounter with others must resist the temptation to be imperialistic and offered from a place of power. Holistic evangelism is a true sharing and so must be our hospitality, as recipients as well as givers.

Mission Snapshot: While ministering in Arlington, Andy and Abby Miller sought to build bridges between the local corps and the Family Life Centre (housing program). They committed to work together to practice holistic hospitality. The key groups who collaborated were the Corps, the advisory group, the housing center staff, and the residents. They met to discuss ways in which they could work together and implement a theology of hospitality. They came up with a range of ideas and decisions which were simple but profound. First was a decision to refer to the families who stayed in the shelter as guests rather than clients or residents. Names matter. Guests are honored visitors who are cared for and welcomed with love

17. Pohl, "Hospitality," 34.

and grace. Room numbers had been a primary identification in the house but it was decided that they would be eliminated. In their place they use biblical names such as the Grace Room or the Barnabas Room. Further, the common area was called the Living Room. It became an important place for sharing, welcome, and relationship building. The verse, "Come to me, all you who are weary and burdened and I will give you rest" (Matt 11:28) was affixed on one of the steps in the shelter. It offered a promise of true holistic Christian hospitality. Everyone connected to the Arlington Salvation Army was committed to living out Jesus mandate. Christian hospitality, which is biblically rich and historically grounded, became the common unifying vision. *Andy Miller III, Arlington, Texas.*

Hospitality is a multifaceted activity. We said earlier that our practice of hospitality makes a theological statement. When we share a table with diverse people we are demonstrating the eschatological vision of the time when all tribes and nations share together in community and worship. In the chapter on the church's story from section 1 we saw how the shared table was a powerful witness to the people in the first century. People who were divided by the wider culture were genuinely connected in mutual relationships in the church. In breaking down cultural barriers the church was revolutionary and attractive.

It is important to remember that hospitality does not need excess and it is debased if it becomes a place of culinary or social one-upmanship. Simplicity is a good guide and will help us retain awareness of the lack faced by so many. In a later chapter, we will consider the question of stewardship in a world of great need. It is important to demonstrate the restraint which celebrates, but does not boast, of joyous sharing without gluttony.

Conclusion

A mission-shaped church announces the reign of God through Christ, demonstrates the reign of God through Christ and embodies mission in the way of Jesus locally and globally.[18] This includes the call to offer regular opportunities to respond to the call of the gospel. It embodies the gospel in compassionate service and generous living. Finally, it calls us to the ongoing life of faith. Every follower of Jesus is called to a lifetime of learning,

18. Frost, *Road to Missional*, 61.

growing and transformation. Conversion is not a momentary event, it is a process. It happens through the "acquisition of a way of life that is embodied and passed along in community . . . also known as the formation of Christ in believers."[19] We invite others to the journey of faith, a journey we ourselves are on. Everyone is welcome to fullness of life, to transformation, belonging, and joy. The kingdom of God has been likened to a banquet to which all are welcome (see Luke 14:15–23; Rev 19:6–9). The image for the end times is a table where strangers become guests and guests become family. We are called today to be part of this banquet and our witness in word and deed says, come to the party. Here there is room for all.

To Learn More:

- *Holistic Hospitality: A Bridge to a Future Army*, by Andy Miller III.
- *Evangelism after Christendom: The Theology and Practice of Christian Witness*, by Bryan Stone.
- *Ancient-Future Evangelism: Making Your Church a Faith-Forming Community*, by Robert Webber.

Toolbox:

- Write out your own story of faith so you feel more confident to share it when the opportunity arises.
- Search online Verge Network for resources on hospitality.

---

19. Stone, *Evangelism after Christendom*, 259.

Chapter Eight

Being Integrated

THE BACK OF A cart under a gum tree in the Adelaide Botanic Gardens provided the inauspicious setting for the start of The Salvation Army in Australia in September 1880. John Gore and Edward Saunders were not trained officers nor were they employed by The Salvation Army. As recent immigrants, they were acting out of their own conviction that The Salvation Army was needed in their new homeland. They were people of faith responding by conviction to build the kingdom of God. As well as some singing and a proclamation of the good news of Jesus, John Gore extended this invitation: "If there's any man here who hasn't had a meal today let him come home with me."[1] Words and deeds. Meaningful concern for a person's spiritual salvation and a heart for the everyday realities of life. With such an emphasis, The Salvation Army in Australia took its first steps.

Soteriological Supremacy

This holistic approach to mission has not always been embodied in the years since. There has often been a tension between the place of verbal evangelical proclamation and that of working for justice and societal transformation. These debates have sidetracked and hampered the mission of the people of God for much of the last hundred years.

Thankfully, in more recent times these divergent perspectives have come together. However, while theologians are finding common ground,

1. Bolton, *Booth's Drum*, 7.

the reality of mission practice in many local contexts is still deeply divided. Within The Salvation Army also we see these divisions continuing. The arguments of corps mission versus social mission have deeply impacted and divided our movement. Michael Goheen says, "Mission is the whole church taking the whole gospel to the whole person in the whole world."[2] Evangelical and ecumenical traditions are embraced herein. Our challenge is to grasp the best in this unity of word and deed, and reinforce it firmly in our practice. The exciting challenge is to truly be a both/and rather than an either/or people of mission.

Wholes Not Fractions

The struggles for the church in regards to holistic mission are symptomatic of a broader issue of dualistic theology. In grasping the full picture of the *missio Dei* we need to move beyond the arguments around division of body and soul, physical and spiritual, and reclaim a picture of God's concern for the whole. Without deviating too far from our key concerns in a book on mission let us simply name the issue and its history. Christianity grew from the Hebrew tradition, which embraces a broad understanding of life as integrated. There are no divisions between physical and spiritual realities. In Hebraic thought all of life was sacred and of interest to God. Somewhat unhelpfully, the Christian church has long been impacted by a dualism which separated a flawed physical world of matter from a more perfect world of spiritual matter. The physical could be sacrificed as the spirit was the ultimate concern.

Dualism has encouraged theologies that emphasize a spiritual salvation as of supreme importance and devalued the earthly context as subsidiary, even irrelevant. With this worldview, the salvation of an individual soul can be given priority even when people suffer hell on earth in their current reality due to the abuse, selfishness and sin of systems and other individuals. Heaven is all that matters and we can ignore the injustice of today if we can get people into heaven. However, what of the concern of God for every aspect of life, indeed all creation, that we have discovered in our story of mission? We have allowed a fraction of salvation to become our focus.

God is interested in wholes, not fractions. All of life, in all its implications inclusive of our spirituality and our physical reality are part of the picture of God's mission. Humanity, and in particular the human soul, is

2. Goheen, *Introducing Christian Mission*, 26.

not the only concern of our creator God who spoke all things into being. Fractional mission—in either direction—is a distraction for the people of God and we are called into a mission of wholeness. Holistic mission seeks to fully embrace Jesus words when he said, "I have come that they may have life, and have it to the full" (John 10:10b).

Salvation for Both Worlds

In our earlier chapter Salvationist Story we noted an evolution of the theology of holistic mission. The article "Salvation for Both Worlds," by William Booth (1889), revealed the extent to which this had progressed. He noted, "I had two gospels of deliverance to preach—one for each world, or rather, one gospel which applied alike to both."[3] The grand scheme for earthly salvation would soon be published in the book *In Darkest England and the Way Out*.

From that point on it should have been implausible for The Salvation Army to narrowly define mission. As a movement, we are inheritors of a broadly focused mission—salvation for both worlds. To neglect either aspect of salvation is to ignore our heritage and offer a fractional vision of Salvationism to the world.

The breadth of this mission is critical. Retreat from one or the other is possible and often common. Holistic mission cannot conceive of spiritual salvation without a concern for the needs of this world, nor indeed a stand for social justice and reform that ignores spiritual concerns. As William Booth said when faced with those who wanted the social work of the Army without the spiritual work, "If you want my social work, you have got to have my religion; they are joined together like the Siamese twins, to divide them is to slay them."[4] When reflecting on this quote Needham observes that "for the church in mission, evangelism and social action go hand in hand. Otherwise, the gospel is perverted."[5]

Beyond Simple Responses

Today language based around salvation for two worlds may be overly simplistic. The first emphasis is clear. It offers an evangelical engagement of the good news aimed at helping people discover eternal hope through Jesus.

3. Booth, "Salvation for Both Worlds," 2.
4. Needham, *Community in Mission*, 63.
5. Ibid.

However, sometimes the second emphasis has been minimized. It has been limited to that of social welfare, or charitable concern for our fellow human beings. Social welfare or charity is far from a full expression of mission conveyed through our deeds. To feed the hungry is critical, but what of the fight against unjust practices and societal systems that have made that person hungry? Even that is not far enough. We must consider our response to the degradation of God's created world which has led to failure of farming practices leading to hunger. The complexities extend further. What of societies continued use of damaging technologies leading to global warming and other long-term damage? These are permanently changing the capacity of certain land to even be farmed and support life. Welfare, social reformation responses, environmental concern and activism all become dimensions of our salvation concern for this earthly world. Mission in deed and activism. The Hebrew Bible prophets from thousands of years ago echo down the years and remind us of the deep connectedness of all dimensions of life and faith.

Mission Snapshot: Our corps in Skelleftehamn is a small corps of about thirty soldiers in a small town of about three thousand people in the northern part of Sweden. For the past fifteen years we have supported immigrants in the area. In recent times the number of asylum seekers has increased. We seek ways to support and build friendships with the asylum seekers in our town. Members of the corps offer Swedish classes. Since we do not speak the native languages of the asylum seekers it is not always easy, but often amusing. We try to teach things to make their life easier, such as greetings, names for food, clothes and other everyday words. For obvious reasons, it's is hard to communicate with the people we meet, but Google Translate is a great help. We know that it means a lot to people to simply have somewhere safe to be and someone that cares about them. In the evening after the language class we hold a "cultural cafe." This is basically a place and time when people can just come and hang out, play games, talk and drink coffee. It's always very interesting. Last year we also conducted swimming classes with women who couldn't swim. Thankfully, now they can swim. We also try to help people with filling in official paperwork, medical appointments and shopping. Basically, we try to be good friends. *Erik Johansson, Skelleftehamn, Sweden.*

Integral Mission

One of the traps in using the term holistic mission is that sometimes it is taken to refer to everything else other than evangelism or spoken witness. This is not helpful and our emphasis upon salvation for both worlds hopefully counters this. But division is still apparent.

In recent years, another term, integral mission, has come into usage arising from a Latin American context. A gathering of Christian leaders, theologians and practitioners as part of the Micah network in England in 2001 offered this helpful definition:

> Integral mission or holistic transformation is the proclamation and demonstration of the gospel. It is not simply that evangelism and social involvement are to be done alongside each other. Rather, in integral mission our proclamation has social consequences as we call people to love and repentance in all areas of life. And our social involvement has evangelistic consequences as we bear witness to the transforming grace of Jesus Christ.[6]

Every word or witness based act of mission cannot necessarily incorporate a deeds component, nor should we expect the opposite. This would be a legalistic response that would undermine true mission. However, the unity of mission needs to be constantly acknowledged. True mission is expressed in a fullness of concern for all aspects of creation, spiritual and material. It is helpful for us to think in terms of integrated responses. As we integrate something we make a new whole by bringing together its various parts. Each individual part isn't in action at all times, but in cooperation and at the right time they contribute and make new possibilities. As people of integral, or integrated, mission we will look for ways to bring the fullness of mission into our encounters. Over time we seek to bring a well-rounded response that expresses the fullness of the kingdom of God, word and deed. Our desire is to bring the full mission of God into people's lives and we integrate different aspects of mission into our practice. It is not our choice to say I am not an evangelist and so I won't witness. Neither can we say I will not perform acts of mercy and will only speak of my hope in Jesus. Integrated mission encourages us, when the time is right, to express the fullness of mission.

In the previous chapter, we considered what it means to be a witness and in our next chapter we will consider being holy, our growth in

6. Micah Network, "Integral Mission," lines 23–27.

discipleship and spiritual maturity. Throughout the rest of this book we will encounter a variety of other ways we express the mission of God. While these are explored individually let us not lose focus on our need to be integrated in mission. May we practice the full mission of the kingdom of God. As we move on with this in mind let us consider justice and activism.

Justice and Activism

God requires mercy and justice. This includes the compassionate action of the responder as well as the passionate activism of the reformer. Internationally The Salvation Army is a leader in response to human need and suffering. Our commitment to alleviating human suffering in multiple ways and multiple locations is without question. Mission in action. The natural companion of social welfare is social activism and reform. Early Salvationists were at the forefront of campaigns to both help the needy and also challenged structures and systems which put people down and kept them there. We knew how to be reformers as well as responders. Today we need to ensure that dynamic interplay continues.

The deeds of mission begin with you and me. Sometimes this can appear overwhelming for us but there are small steps we can take to educate and empower ourselves for living out justice.

Engage with the world around you with eyes attuned to injustice. This means we need to educate ourselves about issues and learn all that we can to enable us to make sound godly responses to injustice. This can be as simple as reading the paper and watching the news to become aware of current issues. It can be as local as observing who in your community is being excluded or denigrated. It can be as global as observing the worldwide news of refugee movements or people trafficking. Key groups can aid us on this journey with a range of groups operating locally and globally. If you are not sure where to start, try an internet search using the key term "social justice organizations."

Next, get active. This will depend upon the issues that are currently relevant and most appropriate to your locality. Again, education will help with ideas for action but in a broad sense there are many ways we can seek to live a more just lifestyle. Shopping ethically will ensure that your comfort and needs are not contributing to the oppression or enslavement of people in other parts of the world. Living more simply can eliminate excess that oppresses others, but then it also frees resources so that you can financially give to fight injustice. Choose a cause and find reputable non-government or faith based agencies that respond to important issues and give financially to support their work. Live generously also in response to disaster situations in other parts of the world, and as an ongoing action consider a regular discipline of sponsoring a family or village. We will explore these ideas further in our later chapter on Being Stewards.

Advocate for the oppressed. On a global scale, need often appears overwhelming. Sometimes the sheer scale of the problem contributes to the continuation and growth of injustice. It is so big that individuals decide there is nothing we can do. As John F. Kennedy said, "The only thing necessary for the triumph of evil is for good men to do nothing."[7] Many individuals can make a difference. Advocacy campaigns have shown the impact of combined numbers in influencing change on both political leaders and corporations. Choose causes that you can bring your faith and sense of God's kingdom values to bear upon. While advocating, take the opportunity to encourage others to do the same, be an educator.

Get involved. Justice and activism is not a spectator sport. As people who are serious about the *missio Dei* there are implications which should emerge in a variety of aspects of our lives. This might be as local as our own corps and neighborhoods, or as broad as national and international responses by The Salvation Army, and even challenging global political issues and ongoing systematic injustice. Don't be a spectator; be prepared to count the cost of involvement. In the chapter on being globally engaged we will consider this topic again. It is important enough to look at more than once.

Mission Snapshot: In 2011, two Salvation Army soldiers from Ilford Corps, East London undertook important research in their neighborhood. They counted the number of people living on the streets. They discovered a man sleeping in a graveyard and as they talked it became clear that they had little support to offer. They left feeling powerless and weak. As they discussed the situation, anger at the way things were awoke within them. They finished that night with a determination to go and do something. By the next winter a night shelter opened. They were determined do more and to look beyond the immediate needs to the root cause. That same year, down the road at Stepney Corps, the issue of affordable housing was becoming a greater need. Person after

7. In this speech before the Canadian parliament in 1961 US president John F. Kennedy attributes these words to Irish statesman and philosopher Edmund Burke. Kennedy, "Address before Canadian," lines 195–96.

person connecting with the corps would tell the same story ending with "we just can't afford to live here anymore." In an area of high deprivation this "social cleansing" was a scandal that corps members couldn't ignore. The two corps soon found themselves in the same room discussing solutions to East London's housing crisis. Other faith organizations, community and civil institutions shared their concerns and joined the conversation through a community organizing alliance called Citizens UK. Together they hatched a plan of affordable housing called "Community Land Trusts" (CLTs) which puts land into shared ownership. This vastly reduces the costs of rents and property prices even in areas of high value. Over the next few years they identified a site, negotiated with councils, London's mayor, and property developers. In 2014 they won the bid for the UK's first ever urban CLT. The result was permanently and genuinely affordable housing for those living on low incomes for generations to come. Hallelujah! Of course, one site is not enough. Now the corps, knowing what is possible, continues the fight alongside their allies. In 2015 they successfully negotiated with their local councils to develop new CLTs in their boroughs. The work continues. *Nick Coke and John Clifton, London, UK.*

Counting the Personal Cost of Justice

Social justice activism comes with a cost. It is not simply the cost of fair trade chocolate or ethically sourced clothing. It is the cost of committing our lives to something far greater than ourselves. Justice requires those who have wealth, education, opportunity, power and hope to utilize, and thereby sacrifice, those advantages so that others might find similar opportunity and life. This is building the kingdom of God. Ken Wytsma in his book *Pursuing Justice* reminds us:

> One of the best things I've read in Dietrich Bonhoeffer is his plain reminder, "When Christ calls a man, he bids him come and die." It's one of the most elemental statements of this simple truth: for Christians having all our needs, wants, and wishes met in this life is not the chief end. We were made for another kingdom. Jesus seems to be calling us to something very different with His invitation "Take up your cross, and follow me" (Matt 16:24 NLT).[8]

8. Wytsma, *Pursuing Justice*, 279.

As people of faith, standing for justice means being prepared to die to self. Chiune Sugihara served as the Japanese consul-general to Lithuania when in July 1940 he was overwhelmed by Polish Jewish refugees who were desperately fleeing the advance of the Nazis. They were seeking Japanese visas as a chance to escape. He contacted his government in Tokyo multiple times seeking permission to provide the visas; each time it was rejected. He had to choose between his dream of a successful diplomatic career and a just response for the oppressed.

Sugihara chose to disobey orders. For twenty-nine days, assisted by his wife Yukiko, he wrote visas by hand. They did all they could to issue as many visas as possible until he was recalled to the Japanese embassy in Berlin. As a final act, he left his official visa stamp with a refugee in the hope that even more could be saved. At least 3,500 Jews escaped the holocaust as a result, with some estimates as high as 10,000.

At the end of the war he was dismissed from the diplomatic service and he struggled to find meaningful jobs for the rest of his life. Many years later when his story was told in book and film, his son was asked, "How did your father feel about his choice?" His answer: "My father's life was fulfilled. When God needed him to do the right thing, he was available to do it."[9]

Mission and God's Creation

Perhaps the last point of contention for holistic mission is the created world. We will explore this subject again in the chapter on being stewards, however it also belongs in any discussion on holistic mission. We value salvation for humankind, salvation from oppression and societal injustice, but can we also see mission in how we care for the environment? Paul declares in Rom 8:22: "We know that the whole creation has been groaning as in the pains of childbirth right up to the present time." The created world in its entirety feels the impact of sin and evil and as such all creation waits for redemption, not simply humanity. Dr. Mick Pope, a meteorologist and theologian, states, "The gospel is broader than 'me and Jesus' because God is involved with the whole of creation, not just human beings. Eco-missiology is concern for creation because God saves us *with* and not *from* creation."[10]

Matthew Seaman notes that evangelicals are the least environmentally concerned among Christians. He suggests this might be due to the impacts

9. Yad Vashem, "Chiune Sempo Sugihara, Japan."
10. Pope, "Preaching to the Birds," 3.

of end-times ideology, pessimism about reform, a strong focus on soul-saving, and even prosperity theology.[11] Eco-missiology remains the least practiced and explored aspect of holistic Salvationist mission. Seaman says that this has not always been the case and has identified a significant pro-environmental praxis in early Salvationism as well as encouraging current pockets of practice and concern.[12]

There is a challenge to take seriously the implications for all creation in our approach to mission. Building the kingdom of God implores us to show deep concern for the created world and to proactively practice creation care through lifestyle choices and activism. To ignore it is to overlook an important focus of concern for our creator God.

> To be *in* Christ means that we can no longer look at any creature in terms of political maneuvering, economic profitability or self-enhancement. If everything has become new because we now behold and engage it *through* him, then literally everything is wrapped up within God's creating, healing, feeding and reconciling ways. In Christ every person is a child of God, and every created thing is God's gift to be protected, nurtured, shared and celebrated.[13]

Conclusion

God desires the redemption of the whole of his creation. The interest is not in fractions, or segments, or simply earthly injustice, or even only human souls. As Michael Goheen so aptly describes it, "All of human life arises from creation; all of human life has been devastated by human rebellion; all of human life, including the social and cultural dimensions, is being restored in Jesus and by the work of his Spirit. The church is the community called to make known this comprehensive restoration in its words and deeds."[14] Fractional mission is a minimization for the people of God who are called to a mission of wholeness. Living out truly holistic mission allows us to act in tune with the intentions of God for the whole created order. It is our inheritance as Salvationists. It is our challenge today.

11. Seaman, "Dark Green Religion," 141.
12. Seaman, "Recapturing a Salvationist Vision," 100.
13. Bahnson and Wirzba, *Making Peace with the Land*, 17.
14. Goheen, *Introducing Christian Mission*, 258.

To Learn More:

- *When Justice Is the Measure*, by Christine MacMillan, Don Posterski and James Read.
- *Pursuing Justice: The Call to Live and Die for Bigger Things*, by Ken Wytsma.
- *Surprise the World*, by Michael Frost.

Toolbox:

- Search for downloadable Bible Study called *Jesus and Justice* from The Salvation Army International Social Justice Commission.
- Justsalvos.com.
- theology-centre.org.uk. Of special interest is the publication "Marching to Justice."

CHAPTER NINE

Being Holy

EARLY IN MY MINISTRY as a Salvation Army officer I met a wonderful lady who was a picture of what it means to live a fully cohesive holy life. She made no claims to greatness, never indulged in overtly spiritualized talk that could appear to set her apart. In fact, in many ways she was simple and ordinary. All she had ever done was to live a life that to her mind was modelled after the example of Jesus. When I met her she was late in years and could have easily been overlooked as just another old soldier who was past any capacity to make an impact. She never spoke of what she had done in life so at first I simply knew her as a humble, obviously spiritual lady.

What I discovered over time was that every second person I met in this country town had been touched by her life. I still don't know how she did it but over decades of simple straightforward living by the values of the kingdom of God she had impacted many people. They were grateful for her influence, for her wise words of faith and Jesus, and for her practically demonstrated love and care. They all knew her, they were all thankful for her impact, and they had encountered a little corner of God's kingdom in her presence. Many would have termed her saintly, due in equal parts to who she was and what she did. She demonstrated missional holiness in action.

Holy Isolation or Holy Impact?

The Salvation Army is part of the holiness tradition, and this remains important to us today. Holiness can conjure up ideas of isolation and personal piety. It can be limited to a private and personal thing rather than a corporate act of spirituality. This overlooks the connection of holiness with transformational impact on the world around us. Perhaps I didn't listen properly to all those holiness sermons when I was growing up, but they left with me the lasting image that holiness was measured by all the things we don't do rather than what we actually do. Don't smoke, don't drink, don't go to the wrong kind of places and don't hang out with others who do any of these questionable things. The message was that you are a holy people and you should isolate yourself from the world around you.

Holiness as prohibition and isolation easily becomes negative and we ultimately see the world as evil and not as God's beautiful creation. We lose sight of the fact that we are here to transform the world for good. If we allow isolation and separation to define our holiness we minimize our potential to build the kingdom of God in the communities in which we are placed. It is a holiness of retreat not of transformational influence. It fails to capture the grand vision of our mission hearted God who desires fullness of life for all creation. We need to move beyond concepts of holiness that disengage us from God's mission.

In Matt 22:35–39 there is a telling encounter between a religious expert and Jesus: "One of them, an expert in the law, tested him with this question: "Teacher, which is the greatest commandment in the Law?" Jesus replied: "Love the Lord your God with all your heart and with all your soul and with all your mind." This is the first and greatest commandment. And the second is like it: "Love your neighbor as yourself."[1]

The question was designed to trick and expose Jesus as unworthy, incompatible with what it meant at that time to be a holy person. Jesus transforms this question about legalism into a statement about love and fullness of life. The first half of the response would have been very familiar to the Jewish religious scholar. Jesus quotes from Deut 6:5, part of the *Shema*, a central prayer for Jews and often the first Scripture taught to their children. Many would recite these words morning and night. Even today they can be found attached to the doorposts of Jewish homes or worn enclosed in a box on their forehead and arm for prayer. Jesus defines the centrality of holiness and faith as a deep and all-encompassing love for God. Then he requires

---

1. Versions of this exchange appear in each of the synoptic gospels, Mark 12:28–31, Luke 10:25–29. Luke's account leads directly into the parable of the Good Samaritan as Jesus' answer to a follow-up question, "And who is my neighbor?" The extreme extent of loving neighbor becomes evident as the story unfolds and the normally excluded and despised Samaritan is praised, not just as neighbor, but indeed as one who expresses God's love.

another step for holy living, love your neighbor as yourself. True holiness is expressed through deep love for God and full love for our neighbors.

Our relationship with God and holiness of life is directly connected with the world around us, in other words with mission. Love God, love others. It's as simple and as complicated as that. We need to note the active focus of the words of Jesus. Jesus did not say, "Abstain from treating your neighbor poorly." Holiness is active. Love God and love your neighbor invites us to the work of transforming this world with the love of God expressed to those around us. To be a holy people calls us to be people active in mission. This is fully cohesive holiness, missional holiness. Deep love for God and full love for others.

Perfect Love

Wesley, and subsequently the Booths, saw the intimate links between loving others and a life of holiness. One of the terms that Wesley coined in explaining holiness was "perfect love." The current edition of The Salvation Army Handbook of Doctrine describes it this way:

> "Perfect love" is perhaps the most comprehensive description of holiness. . . . Through his sanctifying power, the Holy Spirit fills us with God's perfect love, so that we begin to love, not with our own, seriously flawed love, but with the unselfish love of Christ. We are thereby equipped for the path of fulfilling Christ's commandment: "Love the Lord your God with all your heart and with all your soul and with all your strength and with all your mind" and "love your neighbor as yourself" (Luke 10:27).[2]

The more intimate we become with God the more we overflow with the perfect love of God. This love changes us and as a result impacts others and society around us. For Wesley, social involvement was a distinct component of holiness. He challenged people to acts of mercy, feeding the hungry or visiting those who were sick or in prison, as necessary components of the process of holy living.[3] Donald Burke said that "perfect love" within Wesleyan holiness "accounted for much evangelical involvement with the disinherited of society. This is a love which is willing to sacrifice freely of

---

2. Salvation Army, *Handbook of Doctrine*, 205.
3. Needham, "Toward a Re-integration," 129–30.

itself. It is a love which places the well-being of others before personal comfort. Often it appears to be a love which knows no bounds."[4]

Missional acts, in word and in deed, are a natural outworking of "perfect love" and form a foundation of our holiness teaching. Conversely an absence of missional action can act as a diagnostic tool for our life of holiness. Have I loved enough? Does my love for God overflow in love for people and the created world? Does my life express holiness by living out love-infused mission? We are only truly a holy people as we are a missional people. Love for God, love for others. Living a fully cohesive life of holiness.

> **Mission Snapshot:** Mr. and Mrs. Sibby have had a remarkable ministry in Papua New Guinea. Both came from poor families and did not have much opportunity to undertake formal education. They are Salvationists who wanted to be officers but their limited education was a barrier to this ministry. They determined not to let that stop them serving God. Eight years ago they bought land at a place called Back Road. They started a Sunday school and church, but God had more in store. One night Mrs. Sibby had a vision of the boys from the settlement (poor neighborhood) coming and the very next day some of these boys came to Back Road. So they fed them and looked after them and the "House of Hope" began. They look after the boys who come, many of whom are addicts. They receive food for the body and faith for the soul. They now have a chicken project. Boys learn to look after day old chicks, build their own chook houses, and then sell them to support the ministry. Many boys who have come now have jobs, some are married. Lives are transformed each day. There are no pensions in PNG, not much money at all really and when Mrs. Sibby is asked how the resources come, she answers, "Through prayer." Food is given as an answer to prayer on a regular basis. God is always at the center for Mr. and Mrs. Sibby. They are never too tired or busy to pray. They are prayer warriors who live, "Heart to God and hand to man" in beautiful and practical ways. *Miriam Gluyas, Papua New Guinea.*

Social Holiness

At times, Wesley has been quoted in conjunction with a call to missional, activist holiness. "The gospel of Christ knows no religion, but social; no

---

4. Burke, "Wesleyan View," 28.

holiness but social holiness."[5] However, it is a misinterpretation to use "social holiness" as a direct equivalent to social action as holiness. Rather "social holiness" forms the foundation for social justice and reform. As Howard Snyder says, "By 'social holiness' Wesley meant the experience and demonstration of the character of Jesus Christ *in Christian community*, the church. . . . Holiness (the character of Christ) is not solitary or lone or individualistic sanctity but a social (that is, relational) experience based on our relationship with God the Trinity and experienced, refined, and lived out jointly in Christian community."[6] Holiness is practiced in community. Communal life calls us to work for fullness of life not simply for ourselves but for all those around us. Dean Flemming in his book *Recovering the Full Mission of God* outlines the dynamic impact of such a communal perspective on holiness. "The beauty of holiness attracts outsiders into the family of God. This happens when the church's public and communal life wears the brand of Jesus' self-giving love. . . . The church's internal life as a loving, obedient community simply cannot be wrenched from its witness to others. We live out our shared life of holiness in front of the world."[7]

Perfect love, shown in communal social holiness, is indeed a powerful witness to others around us. The holy love of God will be expressed through the holy lives of transformed people. They are prepared to sacrificially love, so that others might find fullness. That is holiness, missional holiness in action. That is who we are called to be.

Nourishment for the Journey

One of the traps for many of us who are activists by nature is to neglect the nurture of our own spiritual life and holiness. It is easy to become so absorbed with mission that we weaken our point of connection with the One in whose mission we are partners in. As Helland and Hjalmarson note in their book *Missional Spirituality*, "Without a missional spirituality, we run the risk of becoming mere activists who simply engage in community service, justice-making or overseas mission projects."[8] The passage from Matthew 22 has already reminded us: love God and love others. God is the

5. Wesley, *Works of John Wesley*, 321.
6. Snyder, *Yes in Christ*, 64.
7. Flemming, *Recovering the Full Mission of God*, 269.
8. Helland and Hjalmarson, *Missional Spirituality*, 25.

source. The perfect love of God working through us is the true empowerment for mission and so we need to nurture our spiritual lives.

Our earlier concerns about dualistic spirituality arise again. A pious holiness only concerned with internalized spiritual concepts or an activist stance intensely focused on earthly human need are both inadequate for a cohesive missional holiness. Principles of incarnation are critical here. When Jesus himself became flesh and entered our human existence he did not relinquish his reliance upon God. Time and again we see a discipline and a pattern to the spirituality of Jesus. He would retreat in prayer and reflection and then emerge equipped for mission. As Robert Webber observes, "The Scriptures and early church fathers teach that spirituality is grounded in God's embrace of our human condition. . . . Jesus is not only the sacrifice for our sin, the victor over death for us, he is also the perfect example of the one who lives in full union with the embrace of God."[9] The rhythm and reliance we see in Jesus is a model for us to emulate.

Dallas Willard, a teacher of spirituality in Protestant circles, speaks of the need to take our guidance from Jesus. He says, first we learn from Jesus about who we are and what we are here for, our place and our ongoing presence in God's eternal purposes. Second, he teaches us about true character or the "good heart" and the importance of compassion, purity and goodwill. Finally, Jesus invites us to follow him in the practices of spiritual disciplines such as solitude, study, silence, service and worship and helps us to see that in our day-to-day activities we act in his name.[10]

Mission Snapshot: At my graduation from William Booth House drug and alcohol rehabilitation program I started with these words: "Hi, my name is Nick and I'm an addict, but by the grace of God I'm more than that today." When I was new to the program, and heard others use that phrase in their graduation speeches, I thought I would struggle to do the same. I was a self-avowed atheist and was not sure the spiritual aspects of the program could be reconciled with my worldview. The manager, Major Bob, often spoke of a "God-shaped hole in the human psyche," one that can only be filled by belief in a higher power. This idea is from the writings of the French philosopher, Pascal. He spoke of the emptiness inherent in the human condition and that people try to fill this void with things around them. This ultimately fails since the infinite abyss can be only be filled with an infinite and immutable object, in other

9. Webber, *Divine Embrace*, 195.

10. Willard, *Great Omission*, 20–22.

words by God himself. From my own experience, and from others in re-habilitation, it is my belief that addicts suffer powerfully from this sense of emptiness, strangeness and detachment. That is why I have come to understand God's central role in my recovery. Step three says we "turn our will and our lives over to the care of God of our own understand-ing." Despite the fact that understanding God seems so impossible, we need to be open to the concept of God. Our ideas are shaped by our individual histories, cultures and personal ideas, so they are going to differ. What is important to me now is not arguing about the existence of God or defining God's nature, but having an open mind and believing that living a life in accordance with spiritual principles leads to a better existence. That, of itself, is a belief in God. *Nick G, Sydney, Australia.*

Tools in Our Backpack

What are some of the tools that can equip us as we seek to emulate the life of Jesus in our walk of missional holiness?

The traditional disciplines of reading Scripture and prayer are crucial. We must resist the temptation to allow this to simply be an internalized and spiritualized process. Our discipline of prayer and Scripture is to change us and as a result to change the world. Earlier in this book we spoke of the need to read Scripture with a missional hermeneutic. We are invited to read Scripture with eyes focused on mission and the overarching story of the engagement of God with humanity and the created world.

In recent years, many have rediscovered the ancient practice of *lectio divina* (divine reading) a Benedictine approach to reading the Bible. Henri Nouwen states his "growing suspicion is that our competitive, productive, skeptical, and sophisticated society inhibits our reading and being read by the Word of God. *Lectio divina* means to read the Bible with reverence and openness to what the Spirit is saying to us in the present moment."[11] Read-ing Scripture in such a way intentionally seeks to allow opportunity for our story and God's story to intersect. The practice involves four stages: read the text, unhurried and multiple times to see what emerges which may be as simple as one word or key phrase; meditate on it, even imaginatively enter into the text, hear it prayerfully as if it is addressed to you; pray it, let prayer arise from your interaction with the Scripture and connection

11. Nouwen, *Spiritual Formation*, xxiii.

with God; contemplate, feel free to linger in the verses and allow God to continue to speak with you through it.

Hellard and Hjalmarson offer a system they term *missio* reading and prayer.[12] They describe a practice of reading Scripture and prayer based upon a missional hermeneutic. We open our lives to the voice of God, with a focus upon obedience to God in our context of mission.

> The Spirit shapes reading in which the mind descends into the heart—from mere information to formation—where God can address and shape us *for the sake of others*. We must embody the text, share the text, pray the text and apply the text in the context of relationships. Eugene Peterson says this "is a way of reading that becomes a way of living" as we foster union with Christ. The Spirit enlivens and directs *missio* reading and prayer relationally as we love God and others from the inside out.[13]

A range of other tools are helpful inclusions in our missional holiness backpack. We would encourage you to explore these further as you discover ways to nurture your practice of deep love for God and full love for others. "New Monasticism" may be a helpful way to nurture our missional life through a reconnection with some of the ancient practices of monastic orders. Chief among these would be through observance of daily office or liturgy of the hours. This is an intentional practice of spending time with God at regular intervals throughout the day to allow for an ongoing rhythm of being in God's presence. Also, let us not forget the classic spiritual disciplines such as solitude, silence, fasting, worship, and confession. Tools such as the Ignatian Prayer of Examen, designed to help us reflect and see the action of God in our day, or John Wesley's Questions for self-examination can be useful to probe spirituality and its outworking in our daily living.[14]

A Walk of Obedience with a Heart of Humility

Eugene Peterson's now classic book on discipleship is titled *A Long Obedience in the Same Direction*. The title itself highlights the final resources in our backpack needed to sustain the journey of missional holiness: obedience and its vital companion, humility. Obedience is not a popular concept

12. Helland and Hjalmarson, *Missional Spirituality*, 112–18.

13. Ibid., 115.

14. See the Toolbox at the end of this chapter for further detail on daily office, classic disciplines, and reflective prayer exercises.

and one that challenges us to the core of our discipleship. Quite simply if we are to read Scripture, reflect prayerfully and seek to practice a variety of spiritual disciplines then the outworking of these will require obedience. In a world of competing ideologies will we be obedient to the voice of God? As Peterson puts it:

> For Christian living demands that we keep our feet on the ground; it also asks us to make a leap of faith. A Christian who stays put is no better than a statue. A person who leaps about constantly is under suspicion of being not a man but a jumping jack. What we require is obedience—the strength to stand and the willingness to leap, and the sense to know when to do which. Which is exactly what we get when an accurate memory of God's ways is combined with a lively hope in his promises.[15]

Obedience. Holiness. Missional living. All these are only possible when we allow our lives to be marked by humility. John Dickson in his book *Humiltas* describes humility as "*the noble choice to forgo your status, deploy your resources or use your influence for the good of others before yourself.* More simply, you could say that the humble person is marked by *a willingness to hold power in service of others.*"[16] Humility is a spiritual discipline because it is a choice, an act of our will or perhaps more rightly a transferal of our will. We set aside our own preference so that our deep love for God and full love for others can be the determining factor in our living. Jesus lived it. He knew the pain of it and the power of it. Here is missional holiness as lived by Jesus:

> Do nothing out of selfish ambition or vain conceit. Rather, in humility value others above yourselves, not looking to your own interests but each of you to the interests of the others. In your relationships with one another, have the same mindset as Christ Jesus:
>
> Who, being in very nature God,
>
> > did not consider equality with God something to be used to his own advantage;
>
> rather, he made himself nothing
>
> > by taking the very nature of a servant,
> >
> > being made in human likeness.
>
> And being found in appearance as a man,

---

15. Peterson, *Long Obedience in the Same Direction*, 171.
16. Dickson, *Humiltas*, 24.

he humbled himself
by becoming obedient to death—
even death on a cross! (Phil 2:3–8)

Conclusion

C. S. Lewis said, "How little people know who think that holiness is dull. When one meets the real thing it is irresistible. If even 10% of the world's population had it, would not the whole world be converted and happy before year's end?"[17] Ideas of holiness which are isolationist or lifeless disregard the true call of the holy life. True holiness is active and draws us towards God and others in profound ways. May we be part of the irresistible 10 percent who in turn draw people towards God and each other.

To Learn More:

- *Missional Spirituality*, by Helland and Hjalmarson.
- *Celebration of Discipline*, by Richard Foster.
- *Sacred Rhythms*, by Ruth Haley Barton.

Toolbox:

- There are many resources you could use to practice daily office. A helpful overview, including reference to other resources, can be found in chapter 8 of Scazzero, *Emotionally healthy spirituality*, 153–73.
- Resources such as Richard Foster's book *Celebration of Discipline* and from the associated *Renovare* group are helpful tools to explore the classic disciplines. Visit renovare.org.
- For intentional reflective prayer tools conduct an Internet search on the Ignatian Prayer of Examen or Wesley's Questions for Self-Examination.

17. Lewis, *Letters to an American Lady*, 11.

Chapter Ten

Being at Worship Together

WORSHIP IS OFTEN USED as a shorthand term referring to the gathering of God's people, mostly on a Sunday and normally in a church building. We sometime even refer to the musicians as our worship team and the singing as the worship time. We risk our understanding of worship becoming very narrow. Paul, on the other hand, suggests a broad definition of worship. "Therefore, I urge you, brothers and sisters, in view of God's mercy, to offer your bodies as a living sacrifice, holy and pleasing to God—this is your true and proper worship" (Rom 12:1). Worship is broad and inclusive of all of our lives. That said, the gathered community of faith is important and corporate missional worship is vital for the people of God. In this chapter, we remain aware of the broader dimensions of worship however are going to focus upon corporate worship. Our intentional gathering for worship can be a missional and formative event.

The early church was encouraged not to give up the habit of meeting together (Heb 10:25). Throughout Christendom corporate worship has occupied a central, often elevated place in the Christian experience. Today, some missional communities question the place of corporate worship. Others are eschewing the gathered community altogether. I would argue that gathering for corporate worship is still an important, transformative and redemptive activity and one which we abandon at great cost. It is also a missional encounter and one we consider vital in the Christian life.

Mission is primarily what God is doing in the world, the church is gathered into God's mission and as such their worship is a witness to that work. We are called to worship where *missio Dei* is central. The outward focus of worship is not that worship itself is evangelism or social action. Rather it is that together we celebrate the mighty deeds of God in the midst of the world as a witness to what God has done and is doing for the sake of the creation. Mission and worship are inseparably and integrally related. "Worship itself is an important locus of mission, a place and time where the people of God celebrate and participate in God's self-giving love for the sake of the world."[1]

In the play, Equus, the psychologist says, "If you don't worship, you'll shrink." Humans are hardwired to worship. Christian corporate worship draws us both towards God and towards each other. When we gather for worship we are actors in this story, not onlookers. It is possible our consumer culture has turned us into spectators when it comes to worship.

> The focus is on my experience, sitting back with arms folded and saying to those leading worship, "Wow me." Do something to grab my attention, catch my interest. They assume worship is like watching a movie; it's something I critique afterward. Can you imagine the Israelites, freshly delivered from slavery, before a mountain that trembles violently with the presence of God (Exod 19), muttering: "We're leaving because we're not singing the songs we like. Like that tambourine song, how come they don't do that tambourine song anymore?"
>
> "I don't like it when Moses leads worship; Aaron's better."
>
> "This is too formal—all that smoke and mystery. I like casual worship."
>
> "It was okay, except for Miriam's dance—too wild, not enough reverence. And I don't like the tambourine."[2]

Worship in which we bring ourselves, focused toward God for the sake of the world, is worship which lifts us beyond our self-seeking agendas and diverts us away from the critiques suggested above. Worship flows from the person and work of God. We worship in response to who God is and therefore the initiator or worship is God and not us. "God always acts first. God approaches us, calls us, and invites us to the holy meeting between himself and his people."[3]

---

1. Meyers, *Missional Worship*, 2.
2. Ortberg and Howell, "Can You Engage," 33.
3. Cherry, *Worship Architect*, 4.

Themes of Missional worship

Missional worship is not about the style, ambience or liturgical pattern of worship. Any church that shapes their worship around the *missio Dei* can be missional. When we gather, the key questions are not if we have the right music, clothing, seating or sermon length, but rather, is our worship shaped around God and orientated to the world? Let us consider some of the ways we might do that as we gather for worship.

Gathering

The very fact of coming together as the people of God is a powerful act in and of itself. When we meet, we say this is important. God is important and others are a vital part of my spiritual journey. Newbiggin says that for Christians, "the weekly gathering for worship is by far the most important thing we do."[4] When Christians gather they come from a diverse range of backgrounds and commit to one another as well as to God. In a previous chapter on the story of the church, we saw how the early church gave radical testimony to the power of Jesus by bringing together people from all walks of life into one community. "The early church broke down the barriers that has been erected in the Roman Empire between rich and poor, male and female, slave and free, Greek and Barbarian, creating a confounding 'sociological impossibility.' . . . The lives of the believing community, nursed and shaped by the biblical story, enabled them to live as resident aliens, as lights in a dark world."[5] The gathered worshipping community is "part of a movement which is both two thousand years old and constantly being renewed."[6] Gathering joins us to millennia of faithful testimony and praise to God. It also shapes us in the here and now as we understand what it means to be a Christ follower today. When we gather, we open ourselves to being repeatedly aligned to the *missio Dei* and then we scatter throughout the week to be salt and light in this world. After we have been together we "know that we are part of something huge—the body of Christ whose solidarity extends across the millennia and across the globe. It is disciplined gathering that produces meaningful scattering."[7]

4. Goheen, *Light to the Nations*, 202.

5. Goheen, *Introducing Christian Mission*, 125.

6. Kreider, *Worship after Christendom*, 133.

7. Ibid., 135.

Praise and Give Thanks

The hymn recorded in Phil 2:6–11 demonstrates that giving honor and praise to God has been part of Christian worship since the earliest of times. Worship confesses that Jesus is Lord and brings glory to God the Father. The *missio Dei* invites people into relationship with God where they are engaged in the *Gloria Dei*, the glorification of God. True worship is God centric. "God wants to be glorified and worshipped, not because he has deficiencies in self-image he is trying to remedy, but rather because he has perfections of character and nature that he wants to display and have acknowledged."[8] Missional worship, while engaged with the world, is God centric. It must never become small and self-seeking. We praise, we give thanks, we enlarge our lives as we lift hearts and voices to the Divine presence.

Telling the Story: God's and Ours

The novel *Watership Down* tells the story of a rabbit, Fiver, who sets out on a journey to escape the impending doom of their rabbit warren and find a new home. Fiver and his little band of followers face many dangers and challenges along the way. Some seem impossible to overcome with their rabbit natures. What sustains and inspires along the way is the simple but powerful act of telling and retelling the story of their folk hero, El-ahrairah. The stories they tell fill them with courage and hope as well as equipping them for the journey ahead. Like the rabbits in *Watership Down*, the people of God are also a story formed community. Our faith is emboldened as we tell and retell the stories of how God has been active in the lives of people throughout the centuries. "The biblical story from Genesis to Revelation is a great drama, a great saga, a play written by the living God and staged in his wonderful creation; and in liturgy . . . we become for a moment not only spectators of this play but also willing participants in it."[9] We tell and retell the story of God, from first creation to new creation, and we are swept up in that grand redemptive narrative. We hear the stories through the readings and through the preaching, through testimony and sharing. Sadly, we cannot hear the whole narrative each time we meet. If we could, we would see God's hand throughout centuries and into our own day and we would

---

8. Hall, *Interplay of Mission and Worship*, 50.

9. Wright, *Freedom and Framework*, 90.

be challenged, confronted and shaped by those stories. In worship, we hear from and are formed by the full sweep of Scripture.

In the tradition of Salvation Army worship, the lectionary does not feature large. Many people value the spontaneity and informality which they believe comes from this decision not to follow set readings each week, however we have lost much by renouncing this rich resource. Reading from the Psalms, the Hebrew Bible, the Gospels, and the Epistles during worship invites the people of God regularly into the grand narrative of God's redemptive work in the world. We have the wonderful privilege of hearing from the full sweep of Scripture when we gather for corporate worship.

Within the grand cosmic narrative of God's actions in the world, there is also space for our own stories. When we gather, we share our own experiences of God in our midst, of God's redemption, grace and love. Our shared stories strengthen us, they encourage and shape us and they call us on in faith and hope. The testimony time in Salvation Army worship has been a blessing to many as we hear how God's story intersects with our own. I once heard General John Gowans refer to the testimony time as one of the most terrifying moments in worship. One never knew what would happen when you open up the platform for anyone to share. He concluded, as many of us have, that it was a terrifying risk worth taking.

World Focused and Transformational

In Amos we hear a stern warning about worship which is self-serving.

> I hate, I despise your religious festivals;
>> your assemblies are a stench to me.
> Even though you bring me burnt offerings and grain offerings,
>> I will not accept them.
> Though you bring choice fellowship offerings,
>> I will have no regard for them.
> Away with the noise of your songs!
>> I will not listen to the music of your harps
> But let justice roll on like a river,
>> Righteousness like a never-failing stream! (Amos 5:21–24)

True worship is focused toward God and orientated to the world. The world is the "ultimate horizon of our calling. We have received the gospel, not simply for our own good, but to communicate it in life, word, and deed. As Israel of old, the church is in need of a worship that directs our lives to the nations. The same elements of liturgy can direct attention either inward on ourselves or outward, orienting us to the nations and our calling."[10] This worship connects Sunday to Monday. Our gathering is not siloed from how we live, drive, spend, work, relate, or give. True worship calls us to be transformed people.

One of the powerful ways that the church keeps the world in its embrace during worship is with prayers of intercession. In some traditions, the intercessory prayers are called the prayers of the people. As we pray the whole church community speaks on behalf of the community and the world seeking justice, love, healing and reconciliation.

Mission Snapshot: Clapton corps is situated in the East End of London. The corps reflects the diverse community in which we are situated and we are deeply connected to our community through both mid-week and Sunday activities. As we gather for worship on a Sunday we start by meeting in the foyer for prayer. As we stand there we look out and see the community for which we are praying. We hear the sounds of the community for which we care and which God has called us to love. Our foyer prayer enacts our belief that Sunday worship is connected to every other day of the week in the community where God has placed us. A recent Facebook update said: The sun is shining, just waiting for evening church at Clapton SA. As we sit here we are aware of the noise that is London, buses, people hurrying past, emergency sirens, people going to the clubs and cafes on the street. The shops up the road that are all open. So glad we can choose to open the doors of the building and pray and be available for our community. *Ruth and Karl Gray, Clapton, UK.*

Culture: Alternative and Parallel

There is often a tension in the Christian life between how much we are called to be contextualized and how much we are called to be different and countercultural. Sometimes we quote Paul in Corinthians saying that we are to be "all things to all people" (1 Cor 9:22) and in the next conversation we skip to Paul's next letter to Corinthians and say we are to "come out from them and be separate" (2 Cor 6:17). This tension exists in our

10. Goheen, *Nourishing our Missional Identity*, 50.

Christian lives and is reflected in how we feel about worship. Dawn says that this tension in worship can be resolved by two words, alternative and parallel. Our corporate worship needs to connect with our culture and offer meaningful engagement with the world. If people experience a disconnect between the worship event and their daily lives it is less likely that they will be able to make the transition from Sunday to Monday. Yet, if our worship only communicates the values and experiences of our culture then it will not be transformative or call us to deep conversion. "To be parallel will deter us from being so alternative that we do not relate to our neighbors; to be alternative prevents our parallelism from moving closer and closer to modes of life alien to the kingdom of God."[11] Worship needs to be parallel and alternative if it is to be authentic Christian worship.

Music is a component in how we express our connection to our culture but also offers critique of some of its values. Luther is well known to have said, "Next to the Word of God, music deserves the highest praise. . . . The gift of language combined with the gift of song was given to man that he should proclaim the Word of God through music."[12] Music has the power to move us deeply, to stir our emotions, to glimpse something beyond ourselves. It has played a part in the cultural life of humankind for millennium. Christians sing our shared faith, we encourage each other and we tell an alternate story to that of popular culture through the words we share. There is contemporary critique in Western churches that some Christian songs are individualistic and overly sentimental. This romanticizing of our relationship with God has been challenged by Michael Frost, who claims, "Jesus ain't my boyfriend."[13] Our love for God should be profound and touch our emotions, however it is not a romantic love but something far more meaningful and far reaching. Music can reflect that love without giving into romantic sentimentality.

Mission Snapshot: The early Salvation Army was known to take well known drinking songs and put Christian words to them to make them easy for people to remember. In 2004 Phil Laeger and Marty Mikles were asked to lead worship at the USA Southern Territory Youth Institute where they reversed tradition and took older profound hymns and gave them new life with contemporary melodies. Along with their own original

11. Dawn, "Worship to Form a Missional Community," 139.

12. Luther, *Luther's Works*, 323.

13. Frost, *Exiles*, 300.

work, this event led to the formation of the musical group, transMission. The name for the group was born out of a passion that Phil Laeger had for the audiences they were seeing as they led them in worship. He wanted the worship experience to be missionally motivating. The name of the group expresses their goal of transforming worship into mission. The recordings of the group are always meant to be a resource and more details of this resource can be found in the toolbox section of this book. Since 2004 transMission has travelled the world and performed for and represented The Salvation Army at hundreds of events with the focus on inspiring worship linked to mission, creating resources and training up new generations of worship leaders. *Bernie Drake, USA.*

Sending Forth

As we conclude our time together in worship we come to the purpose of our worship: the sending out into the world. Schmidt places his chapter on the sending forth first in his book about worship. He argues that the orientation of worship is the world and so the sending forth must guide and shape our time together.[14] "When we are sent forth from the Mass we are sent forth to go out and try again to help transform the world along the lines that God intended and Jesus preached."[15]

In some places, the sending forth has been replaced by a blessing. One of the limitations of this action is that it implies again that the focus of worship is inwards and personal rather than outward and world centered. The verbs chosen for the sending forth are active, with God as their subject and the world as their focus. The people of God are called to go, to love, to serve. It is as we go to love and serve the Lord that our worship is missional. This is the liturgy after the liturgy or as one pastor said, "And now church begins after we leave here."[16]

We are sent out from worship to partner with God in all dimensions of life. This resonates with The Salvation Army's position on the sacraments. The sacraments have arguably been part of Christian worship since the earliest times and in the form we might recognize today from the second century. However, participation in the sacraments is not universal. The Salvation Army is one of the denominations choosing not to partake in the

---

14. Schmidt, *Sent and Gathered.*
15. Pierce, *Mass Is Never Ended*, 38–39.
16. Kreider, *Worship after Christendom*, 164.

tradition of the Eucharist during worship. Sometime after the founding of The Salvation Army, Catherine Booth and George Scott Railton, influenced by the example of the Society of Friends, persuaded General William Booth to reject the use of the sacraments in worship.[17] The precise reasons for this decision were not well documented, leading to a great deal of debate since that time. Much has been written on this topic and there is not room to explore it here, suffice to say that one of the most helpful ways to under-stand our position today is that while not celebrating the Eucharist dur-ing worship, Salvationists are committed to sacramental living. This view suggests that our everyday lives have sacramental possibilities. Our acts of kindness and generosity, our advocacy for justice, our prayer, our worship, are all outward expressions of an inward grace. Phil Needham writes that "the sacramental life is lived in the power of the Spirit. Those who 'walk by the spirit' look for the sacredness of every moment, the presence of God in every encounter, the divine possibility in every human soul. The sacrament in every experience."[18] So we are sent forth from our gathered worship to live lives of engagement with God and with others.

Conclusion

Missional worship is God centric and world focused. Through it we are drawn into an epic story from first creation to new creation. As we con-clude this chapter I share the prayer of sending forth which concludes our weekly service at our church.

> Go out into the world in the power of the Spirit;
> in all things, and at all times remember that Christ is with you;
> make your life your worship
> to the praise and glory of God.
> Amen. [19]

---

17. Sandall, *History of the Salvation Army*, 131.
18. Needham, *Community in Mission*, 19.
19. Uniting Church, *Uniting in Worship*, 668.

To Learn More:

- *Ancient-Future Worship: Proclaiming and Enacting God's Narrative*, by Robert Webber.
- *Missional Worship, Worshipful Mission: Gathering as God's People, Going Out in God's Name*, by Ruth Meyers.
- *Worship and Mission after Christendom*, by Eleanor and Alan Kreider.

Toolbox:

- transMission is a contemporary Salvation Army music group who make resources freely available on www.transmission.virb.com.
- engageworship.org.
- re-worship.blogspot.com.au.

CHAPTER ELEVEN

Being Inclusive

MY HIGH SCHOOL WAS a diverse place and I had friends from all over the world. We had those of Chinese descent whose families came to Australia over a hundred years ago and who sounded just as "Aussie" as I did. Some of my classmates were Vietnamese and East Timorese refugees who had fled war in leaky boats to arrive in this new land. There were second-generation Italians and Greeks full of independence as they sought to break the constraints of parents worried about a culture being lost. Some of my friends were indigenous Australians, who I failed to realize carried the ongoing impact of invasion and theft of their land, language, and culture. Then there were those of Anglo descent like me. A rich and diverse grouping that helped make me the person I am today.

However, church was different. My local Corps was dominated by people who looked and sounded much like me. As I changed location and entered young adulthood my Salvation Army experience narrowed even more and contained almost no heritage other than my own. My world had become strangely white and monocultural.

In earlier chapters of this book we have highlighted the fact that the mission of God knows no borders. The narrative of Scripture constantly challenges the barriers which we as people seem eager to erect. God cares for the all and seeks to cross geographic, cultural, sexual and ethnic barriers. The reminders keep coming, but somehow we miss the point.

Inclusion and Embrace

Inclusion and embrace are embodied in the Godhead. In seeking to understand the triune nature of God the Greek term *perichoresis* is sometimes used. The relationship within the Godhead can be understood like a dance. Three persons make room for each other while also indwelling and becoming one with each other. Relationship within the Trinity is mutual and interdependent.[1] As people made in the image of God we also are created for such inclusive relationship and mutuality. This is the image that Miroslav Volf employs in his masterpiece, *Exclusion and Embrace*. It is at the very essence of God to include the other.[2] He argues that exclusion is a crucial sin and that the appropriate theological and missional response to exclusion is embrace.[3] This is an invitation that calls us to the costly step of enfolding others in the same embrace that we ourselves have found in God. As Volf contends, "The will to give ourselves to others and 'welcome' them, to readjust our identities to make space for them, is prior to any judgment about others, except that of identifying them in their humanity. . . . This will is absolutely indiscriminate and strictly immutable; it transcends the moral mapping of the social world into 'good' and 'evil.'"[4] Our missional God exists by embrace and inclusion; there is no "other."

The Salvation Army *Handbook of Doctrine* reminds us:

> The doctrine [of the Trinity] describes a God-in-community who reaches out to create community. It is the very basis of the inclusive gospel. From its beginning, The Salvation Army has consistently proclaimed this gospel. . . . We seek to include and welcome into the family of God those who feel themselves to be excluded from society. . . . The challenge for us today is to retain that genuine inclusiveness, resisting developments in our corps and centres that may lead people to feel alienated.[5]

Joining God's mission of building the kingdom on earth as in heaven calls and challenges us to model godlike inclusivity. The church, including The Salvation Army, faces significant issues in relation to diversity and

---

1. Salvation Army, *Handbook of Doctrine*, 60. The chapter on the Trinity in the *Handbook of Doctrine* is helpfully entitled "The God Who Is Never Alone."

2. Volf, *Exclusion and Embrace*, 129.

3. Ibid., 29.

4. Ibid.

5. Salvation Army, *Handbook of Doctrine*, 75–76.

inclusion. In particular issues around gender, ethnicity and sexual orientation can appear problematic for us. Let us consider these three as illustra-
tive of the wider issues of inclusion as missional responses.

Gender

The Salvation Army has been proud of its heritage as a movement which,
almost from inception, opened the opportunity for women to preach as
equal to men. We have also long stated that any position in The Salvation
Army, all the way to international leadership as general, is open to anyone
regardless of gender. The 1886 edition of Orders and Regulations for Officers included the astounding stipulation for its time that "the Army refuses
to make any difference between men and women as to rank, authority, and
duties, but opens the highest positions to women as well as men."[6] Early
decades indicate this was reality, at least for some. However, our mythol-
ogy is stronger than reality. Margot Dennis used the somewhat unusual
approach of tracing the status of women officers by examining the nature
of an internal directory, Disposition of Forces, over a one hundred–year period in the Australia Southern Territory. She notes that in early years it only
contained the names of male and single female officers. By 1903 married
females were recognized as a statistic, by 1929 they were recognized by a
typographic character (such as an X) after a married male officer's name. In
1976 the title Mrs. was included with the husband's classification and it was
not until 1995 that a married woman's rank, name and appointment were
all fully acknowledged.[7] Janet Munn quotes a recent international report
on senior leadership in The Salvation Army: "As of 2011, women held 9.07
percent of the command appointments [senior influential leadership roles]
worldwide; married women held 1.73 percent. This is to be compared with
the fact that 53 percent of Salvation Army officers are female."[8] The reality
of full opportunity and inclusion appear elusive.

Claire Emerton, a single woman officer, in *Flawed Folklore* writes:

> I've been struck by the mixed messages our organisation sends its
> women. On the one hand I hear both men and women share folklore
> about the esteemed and equal place of females. . . . [However] I ob-
> serve that the overwhelming majority of senior leadership positions

6. Dennis, *In Her Own Right*, 5.
7. Ibid., 68.
8. Munn, *Theory and Practice of Gender Equality*, 61.

in The Salvation Army are held by men. . . . And I have observed married women officer friends who are taken less seriously than their husbands in certain tasks, merely because of their gender.[9]

It seems that our rhetoric as a movement has not been matched by reality for the women within. Early gender inclusion gave way to a more socially acceptable leaning towards male superiority. While a minority of single women have reached significant roles, the reality for married women has been far less inclusive. Cultural expectations of homemaking have largely overruled equality. Andrew Eason in his book *Women in God's Army* paints a stark reality when he says that "although the Salvation Army provided women with opportunities to preach alongside men, it largely failed to implement sexual equality beyond the pulpit."[10]

If that is the reality for officer women, then what is the situation for females who do not hold organizational rank? Exclusion faced by officer women is symptomatic of wider issues within the movement. This is even more problematic where significant cultural prohibitions inhibit the role of women. Yet even in developed western countries many evidences of discrimination and exclusion persist. God declares that all are equal. As a movement within the body of Christ we seek to emulate full equality. Sadly, the pressures of societal expectations often overrule the values of the kingdom of God. While gender discrimination continues we are less than what the mission of God requires of us. What will it take to truly allow full inclusion for women?

The place of women in The Salvation Army can only be transformed as men and women, all of us, act for change. While I hesitate to say it, men in particular must proactively work for change. Too often (whether as husbands, fathers, corps officers or senior leaders) the decisions of men continue to reinforce gender inequality within The Salvation Army. As Munn notes, "The tendency of empowered leaders to increase and maintain their power over others indicates that those most able to improve a balance of power organizationally are also the least likely to desire such a change."[11] A radical realignment of attitudes, accompanied by actions, will be required.

---

9. Emerton, "Flawed Folklore," 57–58.

10. Eason, *Women in God's Army*, 154.

11. Munn, *Theory and Practice of Gender Equality*, 87.

Within your context of mission ask these questions:

- Are females given equal access to participation in decision-making processes?

- Are females selected for leadership development opportunities?

- Do councils and boards have a number of females proportionate to their wider local involvement?

- Due to historical disadvantage, what steps can you take to advocate in favor of affirmative action to further develop females at all levels of mission and ministry?

- If the broader societal context encourages or requires discrimination against women in what ways are you standing against culture?

Ethnicity

In the 1880s Frederick and Emma Booth-Tucker began the ministry of The Salvation Army in India. In order to share their Christian faith with the local population they took the radical step of assuming the place of *fakirs* or religious beggars who were customarily welcomed among the casteless and those of low caste. "This involved walking barefoot. 'Our English boots were the objects of the keenest criticism, even in the cities, and we soon began to realized that this badge of Western civilization would have to go,' Tucker wrote. It also involved carrying beggars' bowls and living on scraps of food."[12] Booth-Tucker had perceived that his actions created a barrier of ethnic or cultural identity and he did whatever he could to contextualize and communicate in culturally appropriate forms.

As a result of people like the Booth-Tuckers, the early Salvation Army had a confidence to bridge cultural and ethnic boundaries and act in inclusive ways for the sake of the mission of God. At times, we were highly effective in incarnational mission and adapted to a variety of contexts during our period of rapid global expansion. On other occasions the necessity to contextualize was overlooked. The world has changed and the challenge now lies less in reaching out to cultural groups in different lands. Today in many places the world is literally on our doorstep with people of vastly

12 Munn and Collinson, *Insane*, 55

different ethnicities all coexisting in contemporary cities within daily reach of The Salvation Army.

As was my experience growing up the church today is one of the places where integration is weakest. Mark DeYmaz and Harry Li quote research from the United States of America which indicates that the hour of worship on Sunday morning is the most segregated time of the week. There is a predominance of mono-cultural and ethnic specific congregations.[13] I could not confidently speak for The Salvation Army across the globe but certainly in my own context this would also be true. A largely Anglo Salvation Army often isolates itself in worship in an ethnically diverse community. In terms of cultural mix, we are disconnected from our communities and not reflective of the diversity of people around us. The main variance to this pattern appears to be Salvation Army Corps with a particular ethnic focus but who are still monocultural simply in a different form.

Revelation offers a powerful picture of humanity before the throne of God. A picture of God's intent for the kingdom of God on earth as it is in heaven. Visualize this scene:

> I looked, and there before me was a great multitude that no one could count, from every nation, tribe, people and language, standing before the throne and before the Lamb. They were wearing white robes and were holding palm branches in their hands. And they cried out in a loud voice:
> "Salvation belongs to our God,
> who sits on the throne,
> and to the Lamb." (Rev 7:9–10)

There is no setting aside of ethnicity or culture. People of all nations and languages united together in all their diversity and equality in worship before God. As Rodney Woo describes it in his book *The Color of Church*, Revelation 7 "depicts the ultimate worship service composed of all people groups together around the same throne. In anticipation of the racial reunion, God calls his church to prepare for the coming of the Lord. . . . In light of this truth, every worship service at [our church] is our essential groundwork and model for the final convergence of every nation and tribe."[14] How can we remain in cultural enclaves and be true to the challenge of Scripture? The kingdom of God calls us to radical ethnic and cultural inclusion on earth as in heaven.

---

13. DeYmaz, *Ethic Blends*, 23–24.

14. Woo, *Color of Church*, 14.

For decades, church growth theory has been dominated by the homogeneous unit principle. This principle has encouraged a focus upon singular people groups as a more successful way to plant or grow churches. Essentially the principle says like attracts like. Uniformity and cultural similarity make us comfortable and therefore more probable to join a group of like people. DeYmaz challenges this assumption, "Indeed, the question should never have been, *How fast can I grow a church?* Rather, it should have been, as it should be now, *How can I grow a church biblically?*"[15] It is time for us to embrace the biblical image of the people of God, from every nation, tribe, people and language.

Within your context of mission ask these questions:

- What are the different cultural groups in your community?

- Do you know anyone from these cultures? If not, how could you meet them and develop friendships?

- Have you taken intentional steps to learn about the culture, religions, language, and food of other ethnicities in your community?

- What multicultural festivals are celebrated in your area? How can The Salvation Army become involved in a loving and respectful way?

- If the dominant ethnic group in your corps is different to that of your community what steps can you take to close the cultural gap and become more representative of the wider community?

- Have you listened to the stories and struggles of immigrants and refugees in your community?

Mission Snapshot: Berwick Salvation Army in Melbourne includes people from diverse cultures, especially Eastern Africa. This has provided incredible opportunities to engage in mission in different, often challenging ways. It is confronting for a Westerner to be part of traditional African tribal marriage processes that includes negotiating a dowry, or community shaming of a young person who has done something wrong, or going to a community party that starts at 1 a.m. However, all these unusual events allow for a greater depth of shared mission and ministry to take place. Trust is essential to sharing life with people from other cultures. Without it we would never have known of the struggles of a young woman suffering from depression and self-loathing. Nya was experiencing the effects of trauma of

15. DeYmaz, *Building a Healthy Multi-ethnic Church*, 62.

having witnessed war and separation from her family. Her brothers told us that she was sleeping all day and not attending school. For a community who normally hide their difficulties it was a privilege to be told about Nya. We were able to assist and bring her into some of the programs we were offering. She connected with the wider community and began the process of healing. In time, we were able to go with her to see a doctor for her depression, get her tutoring and share as she caught up at school. She started to attend church and joined in all our activities including our study program. Nya finished Year 12, and was accepted into a Para-medicine course at University. This was not only significant for Nya, but also for her community. She is also altering perceptions about African refugees as she contributes to the wider Australian society. *Troy Pittaway, Melbourne, Australia.*

Sexual Orientation and Gender Identity

There is perhaps no more loaded and difficult question facing many in the church today than seeking to understand issues around sexual orientation and gender identity. This book is not the place to debate the biblical texts on homosexuality, nor the research evidence as to the nature and origins of gender identity or same-sex attraction.[16] However, it is a book about the mission of God and we have sought to understand the nature of the radical inclusivity of God's love and grace. This love and grace is for all people including those who identify as LGBTI.[17] As humans we exclude and judge, seeking to distance ourselves from those we perceive as different. Our mission hearted God loves and seeks that all should be a part of the kingdom. There is no "other" in the economy of God.

Untold damage has been done to individuals, who God loves deeply, as a result of theological arguments over sexual attraction and gender identity. To be honest often those arguments are far from theological and are driven by simple agendas of fear and exclusion. Kris Halliday, a gay Salvation Army officer, writes, "Unfortunately, many gay people in many churches are still waiting for actual love and acceptance from their Christian brothers and sisters. Not conditional love, not 'acceptance but . . . ,' just love,

16. A recent publication within a Salvation Army context that explores some of these matters as well as broader questions of human sexuality: Salvation Army, *Honour God with Your Body.*

17. LGBTI stands for lesbian, gay, bisexual, trans* and intersex.

just acceptance, just freedom—the type of love Jesus spoke so wonderfully about."[18] For people who live mission this is not a concept to be debated but people to be loved and accepted.

Within your context of mission ask these questions:

- What messages of exclusion are we extending to LGBTI people and how can we counter these?

- Many Christians assume they do not know any LGBTI persons but statistics tell us otherwise. Do you need to examine your language and speech for prejudice that you may be speaking unaware to LGBTI individuals in your networks, extended family, or church community?

- What steps can you take towards positive engagement with the LGBTI community?

Mission Snapshot: "Why are you here? You hate us!" That was the response to my greeting at the Gay Pride Parade just outside the Training College in Chicago more than twenty-five years ago. The parade wended its way right in front of the campus where I was serving as a young officer. I went with a friend in uniform to hand out candy, greet the folks, and encourage them not to get sunburned that hot day. Conversations with LGBT+ folks still share a common theme: "I hate your Salvation Army!" But it's amazing how many times those conversations end with me returning home later that day to a Friend request on Facebook. Enemies soon become friends when God is involved in the conversation. If I were honest, I think that in many ways we have become the church William Booth walked away from more than a hundred years ago. Snide, sneering, judgmental, rejecting and uncaring to our modern-day "submerged tenth." We've become a gray and dismal misrepresentation of who we should be in God's extraordinary design. We live in one of the most important and exciting times in history. We should be having fun stretching our minds and hearts on this subject. Not fighting back, not sneering, not being afraid of who we are, and certainly not being ugly and hateful. Most Salvationists I know however, officers and soldiers alike, aren't comfortable with this conversation. They become scared, nervous, or even angry when the topic is broached. They wring their hands fretfully bemoaning what is to become of us. They seem to have forgotten that God's simple plan for his called people has never changed: Love. Everyone. There have

18. Halliday, "Making Sense of Scripture," 125.

never been provisos or footnote exceptions. Jesus' simple directive is: "Love your neighbor." And to love we have to be among. Where are gay people hanging out? Why aren't we there loving them for Jesus' sake? For me the answer is simple: "They" are all around me, right here where I live. I have the daily, everywhere-I-go privilege of loving, hugging, smiling, hanging out with, crying with LGBT+ folks on the street and in Starbucks and in bars. I love them! And I love the kingdom privilege they represent. *Stephen Yoder, Chicago, USA.*

Giving Power Away

A crucial step related to inclusion that needs to be confronted is often related to power. Those who are dominant hold power over others, and it is the nature of power that once we have it we do not want to share it or give it away. Leadership after the example of Jesus is servant leadership. It recognizes that true power should only ever be used for others and not for ourselves. Inclusion means utilizing the power in our hands for the sake of those who are marginalized or excluded. Ultimately this means giving power away. In a telling exchange with his disciples about power, leadership and positions of priority in the kingdom of God, Jesus said, "Whoever wants to become great among you must be your servant, and whoever wants to be first must be your slave—just as the Son of Man did not come to be served, but to serve, and to give his life as a ransom for many" (Matt 20:26–28).

For true diversity and inclusion to reign within our corner of God's kingdom are there people who need to relinquish power for the sake of others? Is it time for the dominant voices in our decision-making bodies to relinquish their places? Those dominant voices are often middle aged or older white men. What might it take to give power away? To allow others into roles of influence and leadership. That would be an action of inclusive greatness in the kingdom of God.

All One in Christ Jesus

Over recent years in Australia there seems to have been a resurgence of racism, sexism and discrimination. A situation tragically shared by many other countries as evidenced by the growth of far right political parties. As a person of faith, I must look to the values of the kingdom of God when wrestling with the attitudes of people around me.

The Apostle Paul had to confront a growing exclusivism within the Galatian church. Here was a church that was getting very good at defining who was "in" and who was "out" when it came to the kingdom of God. Their leaders made it clear that if you stayed within their strict religious parameters then you could find a place within the community of God. When you begin to define your religion in that manner it easily becomes a breeding ground for exclusion. If we are in, then obviously, someone else is out of God's love.

Paul had been born as part of the "in" group and had for many years defined himself by religious legalism. Here he writes to the church at Galatia: "So in Christ Jesus you are all children of God through faith, for all of you who were baptized into Christ have clothed yourselves with Christ. There is neither Jew nor Gentile, neither slave nor free, nor is there male and female, for you are all one in Christ Jesus" (Gal 3:26–28).

You are all one. There is no division. All are children of God.

We can see the radical inclusivity of Paul's words. But Paul's words held an even more direct challenge at that time. Jewish men of his day were taught a prayer to use at the start of each day: "I thank God that I am not a Gentile, I thank God I am not a slave, I thank God I am not a woman." Those words may seem extreme but as we look around our society it seems many are still praying prayers like that. Maybe even within the church, within The Salvation Army? Men in particular need to look deep within and confront the discrimination that can be hidden there. This is equally true for all of us: man, woman, culturally dominant group or minority. All of us need to challenge and confront in our own hearts the way we marginalize and exclude people different to ourselves. The word of God inverts the preconception of Paul's day, and ours. There we find the heartbeat of the kingdom of God. We are all one in Christ. Does that same heart beat within us?

In 2012 the chief of the Australian Military, Lt.-General David Morrison, released a statement in response to a sex abuse scandal which went on to become an internet sensation. He made many important points, but one line in particular stays with me: "The standard you walk past is the standard you accept." If we witness inappropriate behavior or attitudes and do nothing about it then we have endorsed it. That endorsement is directly at odds with the mission heart of God. The standard you walk past is the standard you accept.

Conclusion

In her book *The Strength of the Weak*, Dorothee Sölle tells the story of a rabbi who asked his students how they could tell when night ends and day begins:

> "Is it when, from a great distance, you can tell a dog from a sheep?" one student asked. "No," said the rabbi. "Is it when, from a great distance, you can tell a date palm from a fig tree?" another student asked. "No," said the rabbi. "Then when is it?" the students asked. "It is when you look into the face of any human creature and see your brother or your sister there. Until then, night is still with us."[19]

May we look deep into the eyes of others. Different gender, different ethnicity, different sexual orientation, people hurt and marginalized by society. Look deep into their eyes and see our brothers and sisters. As we recognize our shared humanity, that we are all children of God, then through inclusion and embrace we are building the kingdom of God.

To Learn More:

- *Building a Healthy Multi-ethnic Church: Mandate, Commitments and Practices of a Diverse Congregation*, by Mark DeYmaz.
- *Honour God with Your Body: A Christian View of Human Sexuality*, Thought Matters 4, by The Salvation Army Australia.
- *Theory and Practice of Gender Equality in The Salvation Army*, by Janet Munn.

Toolbox:

- Search salvos.org.au for the Inclusion toolkit.
- Search online for Cultural Intelligence or Unconscious Bias resources and training.

19. Sölle, *Strength of the Weak*, 41.

CHAPTER TWELVE

Being Stewards

A while ago I lent a book to a friend. When reading it in the bath one night, she dropped it into the water and while the book was eventually dried out, the pages were swollen and distorted. The first I knew about this accident was when she returned to me a brand-new copy of the book. She said she was too embarrassed to return my original book so badly damaged. I suspect many of us would have done the same. We understand that when we are stewards of another person's property we should treat it with care and return it in the same condition in which we borrowed it.

Everything Is on Loan

This simple idea offers us a metaphor for the expansive topic of stewardship which is an ethic that guides how we care for or manage resources. Christian stewardship is based on the premise that "the earth is the Lord's and everything in it, the world, and all who live in it" (Ps 24:1). It is also informed by the Apostle Paul's rhetorical question, "What do you have that you did not receive?" (1 Cor 4:7). Stewardship is built on the notion of ownership. If everything that we have belongs to God, then we are custodians of all our resources. In light of these ideas we are invited to reflect on how we should live when all our resources are on loan. As partners with God in the world we are called to be faithful stewards of all we have been given. The word which we translate to steward in the New Testament is *oikonomia*. It contains the ideas of the rule, *nomos* and household, *oikos*. Contemporary translations often translate this word as manager or administrator, but in so doing may lose something of the notion of the entrusted leadership contained in the original Greek. The steward may have had responsibility for the house and even rule the household, but it was an entrusted ruler-ship, one executed on behalf of another. Christian ideas of how we live, lead, spend and manage should be shaped through the lens that all things belong to God and we have been entrusted with their care. "Every faculty you have, your power of thinking or of moving your limbs from moment to moment, is given you by God. If you devoted every moment of your whole life exclusively to His service, you could not give Him anything that was not in a sense his own already."[1]

Living missionally is a call to live a life aligned to kingdom values and practices. Stewardship is how we shape our use of resources along those lines. Before going any further, it may be helpful to stop and think about all the resources that you use in a typical week. Here is a short list to get you started, you will no doubt be able to add more. Time, money, energy, talents and skills, education and the environment. In this chapter, we are going to consider two topics in more depth: the environment and consumerism. However, a missional ethic of stewardship invites us to think about how we use all the resources in every aspect of our lives.

The Environment

Christianity has been condemned in the past for promoting an ethic of unfettered dominion over nature. This has led to destruction and terrible environmental damage. Today, however, there is a growing awareness that we have an obligation of responsible stewardship towards God's good cre-ation. We may have been a little late to the party on this important issue, but a Christian concern for the environment is thankfully gaining momentum.

It is not hard to find paradigms for understanding our relationship with the environment throughout Scripture. Walter Brueggemann says that "land is a central, if not the central theme of biblical faith."[2] Scripture affirms divine ownership of the land and the divine gift that the earth is to humankind. Many indigenous people understand land as a gift. The in-digenous people of Australia express this by saying that we do not own the land but the land owns us. This world and all it contains are not commodi-ties to possess but gifts. They are divine gifts from God, who says, "The land

1. Lewis, *Mere Christianity*, 143.
2. Brueggemann, *The Land*, 3.

is mine and you are but aliens and my tenants" (Lev 25:23). These are the key ideas which shape our eco-theology. In the creation story, we see that humans and other animals were all created, blessed and told to multiply. Humans were unique in being created in the image of God. They were given the mandate, to "rule over the fish of the sea and the birds of the air and over every living creature that moves on the face of the ground" (Gen 1:26). This instruction to "rule over the earth" has certainly got us into hot water and possibly "few commands have been more misunderstood than these."[3] A full discussion of these verses is not possible in this chapter, but a few insights might offer a more ecologically sound hermeneutic.

The first of these two commands is *kabash* and is often interpreted as subdue. It is an instruction that they are to use the earth for life and survival. The command was to subdue the untamed land so it becomes fertile. Any farmer would understand that idea, subdue to bring forth life, not subdue unto death. The second term, *radah*, is used elsewhere in the Hebrew Bible in the sense of ruling over, and is often translated as dominion. Again, this is a term which has sometimes been understood as eco-hostile. Yet it is a royal word and refers to the kingly rule. A good monarch rules for the good of their subjects, not their destruction. So, if we apply it to nature we see we are invited to live for the good of the planet and seek its welfare in all we do. "God pronounced his creation 'good'; to [humans] he gives the responsibility to keep it so."[4]

A further idea that has damaged our care of the earth is the belief that this world is only a temporary dwelling with our real home being elsewhere. This idea is coming under increasing scrutiny and there are clear biblical themes that the earth itself is part of our future hope. A hope of a new creation is expressed in Isa 65:17, "Behold, I will create new heavens and a new earth," and expressed again in Rev 21:1, "Then I saw a new heaven and a new earth." Christians not only look back to the creation story but look forward to the new creation which is yet to come. "As is the case with all other aspects of biblical eschatology, what we hope for from God affects how we are to live now and what our objectives should be."[5] Christians are called to order their lives and their missional engagement in view of this hope. Creation care is missional.

3. Moss, *Earth in Our Hands*, 39.

4. Ibid.

5. Wright, *Old Testament Ethics*, 141.

The Lausanne Global Consultation on Creation Care and the Gospel convened in Jamaica in November 2012 and after deep theological and mission reflection, formed two major convictions.

> [First, that Creation Care is indeed a] gospel issue within the lordship of Christ. . . . This is not only biblically justified, but an integral part of our mission and an expression of our worship to God for his wonderful plan of redemption through Jesus Christ. Therefore, our ministry of reconciliation is a matter of great joy and hope and we would care for creation even if it were not in crisis. [Second] we are faced with a crisis that is pressing, urgent, and that must be resolved in our generation. . . . Love for God, our neighbors and the wider creation, as well as our passion for justice, compel us to urgent and prophetic ecological responsibility.[6]

Christians are called to live out responsible stewardship of the environment in a variety of ways. It might be through our worship, through theological reflection, in practical action, advocacy and purchasing decisions as well as local and global action. It is a big task and there is a danger of helplessness arising from a sense of ecological apocalyptic doom. As Christians, we live in the "now and not yet" which gives us reason to live and act in hope. It is this hope which must compel concrete action towards God's good creation.

Consumerism

In 2013 a factory fire in the Rana Plaza factory building in Bangladesh resulted in the death of 1110 people. Global companies were exposed for exploiting workers in harsh and unsafe working conditions. This tragedy threw the spotlight onto the real cost of fashion in the West. The cost others pay is high so that we in the West can buy cheaply and the shareholders can reap large dividends. Of course, this fire wasn't the first evidence that consumerism had resulted in global exploitation, however it did put the issue on the front page of the news for a while. It resulted in the development of the Fire and Building Safety Accord in Bangladesh, which was designed to improve safety and conditions for garment workers.

Every time we consume, we impact others, often unknowingly, but still the impact is real. In a Christmas day sermon in 1967, Martin Luther King explained it this way:

6. Lausanne Movement, "Lausanne Global Consultation," lines 18–35.

It boils down to this, that all life is interrelated. We are all caught in a network of inescapable mutuality, tied into a single garment of destiny. Whatever affects one directly, affects all indirectly. We are made to live together because of the interrelated structure of reality. Did you ever stop to think that you can't leave for your job in the morning without being dependent on most of the world? . . . This is the way our universe is structured, this is its interrelated quality. We aren't going to have peace on earth until we recognize this basic fact of the interrelated structure of all reality.[7]

When we think about stewardship we must consider how our inter-connectedness impacts our consumption. Consumption is no longer a local issue. Vincent Gallagher says that there are seven social sins which are the direct result of consumption in a globalized world. They are sweatshops, exploitation of immigrant workers, slavery, torture and assassination, abuse of God's creation, hunger, child labor, and violence against women. These, he says, are the true cost of low prices.[8] In our search for lower prices and higher profits, we have failed to ensure that workers are protected, rewarded, and work free from the tyranny of modern slavery.

Mission Snapshot: Our consumer choices are often driven by our quest of the cheapest prices and so fair trade is often seen as an optional extra. For me, the choice to "go fair trade" began with chocolate. Some time ago I became aware of the prevalent use of trafficked children in the production of cocoa for most of the world's major chocolate brands. I could not ignore the fact that a crucial ingredient in the profitability of the "harmless" chocolate bar was the literal blood, sweat, and tears of trafficked children. My curiosity grew into an insatiable quest to understand the provenance of products I bought. I became obsessed with seeking out fair trade or ethically certified goods for everything I bought. My commitment to fair trade was all encompassing. It ranged from being part of the launch of a fair trade underwear range in the middle of an English winter (that's a whole other story) to ensuring that our wedding was fair trade, ethical and carbon neutral. Why the obsession? The simplicity of my fair trade lifestyle choice is this: It's a matter of justice. It's a choice I am compelled to make for the sake of people who don't have choice. I do it for the right of every person, wherever they are, to earn a fair day's wage for a fair day's work. My conclusion?

7. King, *Strength to Love*, 69.
8. Gallagher, *True Cost of Low Prices*.

> Sometimes the cheapest deal isn't the best deal, especially for the people that produced that product for you. *Graeme Hodge, London, UK.*

The driving force behind these issues is consumerism. Living missionally asks questions about who we are and how we consume. Brueggemann, a well-known biblical scholar and theologian, has recently collaborated on a book which boldly calls us to depart the consumer culture. He claims that free market ideology permeates much of the West and produces economic crises, violence, and an exhausted planet.[9] As disciples of Jesus our place in the free market economy needs to come under scrutiny. There is a real challenge of those who wish to live missionally when it comes to consumption. We are children of our culture and as such it is hard to critique our own place in this cycle of consumption and its global impacts. However difficult it is we must critique our own assumptions and behaviors and consider their consequences.

A while ago I felt my iPad needed replacing. I had been given it some years earlier and a couple of new models had come and gone in the intervening years. I rely on my iPad for presentations while teaching, so was able to quickly justify this new purchase. While considering my purchase I read Ken Wytsma's book *Pursuing Justice*. I read about the impact of the electronics industry in Africa and the suffering it can cause in the mining of minerals used in much modern technology. He quotes from a short film, *Consuming the Congo*, and calls us to be aware of the impact of our electronics purchases. He highlights the impact on women and children who are caught up in the violence and slavery born from an industry which developed to satiate our need for new devices.[10] I felt challenged and the iPad lasted another eighteen months before it completely failed and was replaced. Missional living does not call us to completely exit the consumer culture, I am not sure if that is possible for most of us. Rather missional living calls us to question how, when, and how much we consume in light of kingdom values.

Ethical Consumption

One way to address the negative impacts of consumerism is to consider our buying patterns and to commit to ethical consumption.

9. Block et al., *An Other Kingdom*.

10. Wytsma, *Pursuing Justice*, 128.

As early as 1888 The Salvation Army in Australia was importing tea from India and selling it to raise funds for their work. This imported tea, known as Hamadova Tea, gave fair profits to the farmers in southern Asia as well as supporting work in Australia.[11] More recently in the 1940s Mennonite Christianity inspired a movement which came to be known as Ten Thousand Villages. This was a forerunner of what we now call Fair trade which is a social movement which seeks both sustainable practices and fairer trading conditions for workers. This movement has been inspired by values such as justice, *shalom*, mutuality, and respect. It seeks a world in which consumerism is not only sustainable, but just.

Fair trade is not one single entity, but rather is a diverse movement who share some common themes and practices. The overall goal is greater equity in international trade and to help consumers make ethical choices. Within fair trade there is a recognized system of labelling to help the consumer make ethical choices. Of course, no system is perfect and there are some limitations of the fair trade labelling system, but it remains one of the most pervasive tools to inform the purchaser about the product they are buying.

The movement for ethical consumerism is far broader than fair trade. Ethical consumption is the goal. This means to consume in a manner which minimizes social and environmental damage and even avoid products if such

Mission Snapshot: In the mid-1990s The Salvation Army rented two small rooms in Old Dhaka. The aim was to help women learn a sewing trade and provide a way out of sexual exploitation. The items they produced formed the stock for the first Sally Ann shop opened in Dhaka. The women were paid for what they made, and attempts were made to find a market for their products. However, sales were not enough to sustain the concept. In 2002, Sally Ann partnered with The Salvation Army in Norway. They changed the design of the products and made them more appealing to the Western market. Within a year Sally Ann opened its first store in Norway. Sally Ann products have since been sold in several countries including permanent stores in Denmark and the United States. Producer countries currently include Bangladesh, Pakistan, Kenya and Moldova. In 2013 Sally Ann changed its name to Others to reach a broader audience and explicitly point toward the reason for its existence. The mission of this project is to fight poverty, to pay

11. This early example of fair trade has given its name to a cafe, the Hamadova Cafe at the Melbourne 614 corps which opened in 2011 in the same building as the original fair trade venture commenced.

> fair wages for fair work, provide safe and clean places of work, promote
> gender equality, give dignity to workers, and to develop self-esteem.
> *Sally Ann (now known as Trade for Hope/Others), Dakar, Bangladesh.*

damage cannot be minimized. Living missionally means being concerned
about our patterns of consumption, knowing how it impacts God's earth and
its people, and then making ethical choices in every purchase we make.

Generosity

Another way to ensure we are good stewards of our resources is to live
generously. Our culture worships possessions and wealth. We strive to own
things and pursue money. Throughout the gospels, Jesus challenges this
ethic constantly. Second to the kingdom of God, the gospels record Jesus
talking most about money and possessions. He knew they posed a danger
in how they would harmfully shape us and oppose kingdom values. He
seemed to suggest that we would worship our wealth or we would worship
God with our wealth, but it's enormously difficult to do both (Luke 16:13).
Worshiping with our wealth is living generously, open-handedly and with
an eye to what we can give rather that what we can receive.

Once a year The Salvation Army makes an appeal to its people, to give
sacrificially in a special offering called the Self Denial Appeal. This appeal
started in the very earliest days of the Army and is now international. From
villages in Papua New Guinea to the suburbs of New York and all across
the globe, Salvationists make generous giving a special focus of their lives
to support the world-wide mission of the Army. The giving is often in addition to the weekly tithes and offerings and for many is truly sacrificial.
In Australia, the appeal is audacious enough to suggest the giving of one
week's salary. The Self Denial appeal is not only a time of financial generosity, but often a time of rich spiritual blessing.

Generous living is biblical and to live redemptively is to live generously. Living with open hands is also transformative. We are reminded that
we do not own things, but that they are a gift from God, and as such, must
be shared with the whole of God's world.

Conclusion

In her novel *Gilead*, Marilynne Robinson says, "Theologians talk about a prevenient grace that precedes grace itself and allows us to accept it. I think there must also be a prevenient courage that allows us to be brave. . . . This courage allows us, as the old men said, to make ourselves useful. It allows us to be generous, which is another way of saying exactly the same thing."[12] Living missionally requires courageous stewardship which takes seriously the notion that everything we find in our hand is a gift and we will be called to account for how we treated that gift on behalf of the world and its inhabitants.

To Learn More:

- *An Other Kingdom: Departing the Consumer Culture*, by Peter Block, Walter Brueggemann, and John McKnight.
- *40 Day Spiritual Journey to a More Generous Life*, by Brian Kluth.

Toolbox:

- wegogreen.ca. Canadian Salvation Army resources for environmental stewardship.
- Search online for resources for ethical shopping. For example, the Baptist Union of Australia's *Behind the Barcode*.
- tradeforhope.com. Website of The Salvation Army fair trade formally known as Others.
- Download the Environmental Justice Pack by Matt Seaman from just-salvos.com.

---

12. Robinson, *Gilead*, 290.

CHAPTER THIRTEEN

Being Global Citizens

I RECENTLY SAW A world globe for sale that invites you to color in the countries you have visited. The goal is to have a fully complete color globe which I assume will make you the envy of all your friends. Many of us would be able to color in some countries other than our own as we are far more mobile than any time in history. Travelling, of course, is not the only way to engage with other countries or cultures. We have the unprecedented opportunity, challenge and privilege to engage with people and cultures from across the world. Technological advancements have increased connections between people more than ever before. Television, movies, social media, and the internet bring the world to us. Globalization has a myriad of consequences. Two of which are the growing proximity of the world's religions to each other and the increasing interdependence of our world.

This chapter intersects with various earlier discussions, so if you have not read this book in a linear way (as I know most of us don't these days), can I suggest you also dip into the chapters on the emerging global story, being integrated and being stewards. In this chapter, we are going to consider global engagement in a couple of different areas. First, we will discuss engaging with other faiths, both at home and abroad. Then we will explore engaging with different nations through travel and online activism.

Engaging with Other Faiths

"No issue is more important, more difficult, more controversial, or more decisive for the days ahead than the theology of religions. . . . This is *the* theological issues for mission in the 1990s and the twenty first century."[1] Christianity has always engaged with other world religions. The earliest followers of Jesus seemed to simultaneously borrow from the religions of the day while also struggling against them. Religious pluralism is not new. By any measure though, our current cultural context has raised the stakes in this area and created levels of engagement never previously known. Migration, mass movements of people, and technology have heightened interaction and engagement in local communities. The major world religions coexist in a way without precedent. This is true culturally and religiously.

Globally "the percentage of the world that is religious continues to increase. . . . Projections to 2020 indicate a sustained decline of the world's nonreligious population. . . . Christianity and Islam dominate religious demographics and will continue to do so into the future . . . [and] religious diversity is increasing in many countries and regions."[2]

So how do we respond to people of other faiths and is there a Christian response to other world religions and their followers? This is a complex question today. It seems that the answers to this question vary on a continuum from one extreme which sees all other religions as iniquitous and deserving of annihilation, to the other end of the spectrum which sees all religions as equally legitimate and deserving of respect and preservation. We might summarize the responses within Christianity to world religions with three positions on a continuum. First, is the exclusivist response which holds that the claims of Christianity are true to the exclusion of other religions and world views. Second, inclusivism says that God was revealed in Jesus however God may be revealed in other religions. This is seen in the idea from Karl Rahner of the "anonymous Christian," referring to an adherent of a religion who is saved through Christ even though they do not know or acknowledge him. Finally, is the idea pluralism which allows space for truth claims in all religious traditions. While an orthodox Christian faith has often been expressed as exclusive, faithful Christians find themselves at various places on this spectrum.

Metaphors for Engagement

So how are we to proceed? John Dickson argues that Christians should be confident to share their faith and also to be willing to explore the other world religions in an open and honest manner. He uses the metaphor of art. He

---

1. Anderson, "Theology of Religions and Missiology," 200.
2. Bellofatto and Johnson "Key Findings of Christianity," 157–58.

asks what an art curator might do if they had a work of inestimable beauty in their collection? "A truly assured curator, that is one with a deep confidence in the excellence of his prized item, would place all the gallery lights on full, confident that as careful art lovers inspect the whole collection, viewing all the works in their best light, one painting, in particular, will draw people's attention."[3] In the book *Encountering World Religions* the authors suggest that we explore our metaphors of mission and ask how they shape our response to other faiths. The metaphor they suggest for encountering other faiths, is that of gift giving.[4] The metaphor of gift suggests that the way of Jesus is a treasure to be shared, not an argument to be won, it is an offer to be made, not a conquest to be accomplished, it is grace driven not victory focused. "Giving a gift is a different kind of activity . . . bringing the gifts of medical care, of education, of Christian community as a tangible expression of the Gift that is Jesus Christ."[5] Whatever the tangible outworking, they are all expressions of "thy kingdom come" in our encounters with others.

At this point, it may be helpful to revisit the concepts of *missio Dei* and kingdom of God explored earlier in the book. These foundational principles lead us to ask what is God doing in the world and how can we be partners in that movement? What do you think God's kingdom looks like in your context and in the broader sweep of our world? If you believe that the kingdom of God is a place that is life giving, just and grace filled, then these things should guide you. What do those principles look like when applied to our encounter with world religions? I guess you get the idea. Our picture of the kingdom of God calls us to seek a world of peace, reconciliation, social harmony and justice. Any encounter we have with people of other faiths must be guided by these principles. There are, however, many Christians today who favor a militaristic or imperialistic view of the kingdom of God. In that worldview, it is not hard to arrive at a missional ethic of overthrow and domination. I recently met a young Christian who advocated the use of violence to defend Christianity even in a normally peaceful Western nation. I can see where that thinking comes from but to be honest find it hard to reconcile with the Jesus I meet in the gospels. Our encounters with world religions and people of other faiths will be guided by our ideas of the kingdom of God and the missional imperative that flows from those beliefs. Love must be our guiding principle.

3. Dickson, *Spectators Guide*, 6.
4. Muck and Adeney, *Christianity Encountering World Religions*, 320.
5. Ibid., 10.

The Cross and the Crescent

Most of us who are old enough can remember where we were when we heard of the 9/11 attacks on the World Trade Centre in New York. We can picture the scenes as those monoliths crumbled. This event brought into sharp focus the intersection between two of the great monotheistic religions of the world: Islam and Christianity. Despite the assertions of popular media, the world's two largest religious faiths have much in common. Our lives are guided by a holy text which share stories of many of the same characters, God is known as provider, creator, sustainer and judge, both assert the place of divine revelation and human moral responsibility.[6] For centuries the "Cross and the Crescent" have peacefully coexisted and enjoyed good relations, however moments of confrontation, conflict and war overshadow the memory of more tolerant times.

In our own day, the growing threat of global terrorism presents us with a challenge to draw on all our "theological resources to develop contemporary models of religious pluralism and tolerance grounded in mutual understanding and respect."[7] This quote comes from Catholic priest Thomas Michel. He has served as director of the Islamic Office of the Vatican Council for inter-religious dialogue. He has also taught Christian theology in Islamic theological faculties in Islamic countries for many years and reflects: "My conclusion after all this time is that what Muslims are really concerned about is very different from anything to do with terrorism or violence, both of which are strongly rejected and opposed by the vast majority of Muslim believers."[8]

So how do we respond personally in our encounter with world religions? I offer the following way forward for Christians in the West who wish to engage with people of other faiths.

- First, there is nothing so powerful in understanding others than to engage with people. Building friendships with people of other faiths will be the best way to learn and engage. The internet and media offer only a slice of the picture. Everything changes when we know people. When a previously abstract idea becomes flesh and blood to us, empathy and understanding grow. This does not necessarily mean we will

---

6. Jenkins, *Next Christendom*, 211.
7. Michel, *Christian View of Islam*, xi.
8. Ibid., 150.

agree, but rather we will develop in our understanding and respect, making our engagement far more meaningful.

- Second, we need to acknowledge that in the past the Christian church has been entwined with political powers. Imperialistically sanctioned violence is in direct contradiction to Jesus teaching. Jesus brought us a new way, the Suffering Servant, the Prince of Peace and as his followers we are called to walk in those footsteps. It is a complete contradiction for the Christian church to endorse violence as a means to share the good news.

- Third, we need to acknowledge that there are many voices in other faiths just as there are in Christianity. Fundamentalist voices in both Islam and Christianity, for example, are barely recognizable to many of their adherents across the world.

- Fourth, engage with those of different faiths. Respectfully admit differences, engage in dialogue, share faith as a gift, tell the story of Jesus in your own life, show kindness and give evidence of the coming kingdom of God in words and deed.

- Finally, if you encounter opposition, then follow Jesus instructions to "love your enemies and do good to those who hate you" (Luke 6:27).

The final vision of the kingdom which is to come is one where people come from all tribes and nations. Ours is not to judge but to love, and we leave the mystery of the final days in the hands of one who is infinitely wiser, more loving and just than we are. Some of our encounter with other faiths and cultures is close to home. People of different cultures live, work, shop, exercise and study alongside of us. However sometimes we encounter difference because we choose to travel and it is to this form of global engagement we now turn our attention.

Mission Snapshot: In 2014 General André Cox became the first-ever Salvation Army general to visit Kuwait. This visit included a meeting with the crown prince that was hailed as a significant moment for all Christians in the region. Early in the visit the general was presented with his own Gutra, the traditional headdress of the region. On the following day, The Salvation Army leaders chose to follow in the tradition of the Booth Tuckers. In India in the 1880s they chose to dress in local garb and in 2014 General Cox did the same. His Highness Sheikh Nawaf Al-Ahmad Al-Jaber Al-Sabah, crown prince of Kuwait welcomed him to the Seif Palace. The meeting between the crown prince and the general was filmed and broadcast on local TV. Reports and pictures featured in newspapers throughout the Gulf countries, encouraging Christians throughout the region. Through this simple, but profound act, General Cox embodied respectful and incarnational mission. *IHQ, London, UK.*

Engaging Abroad

While migration might be bringing people into our neighborhoods, travel is taking us to theirs. Travel opens the doors to encounters that only the most intrepid travelers of previous generations knew. Our capacity to engage, connect and visit countries other than our own is without precedent. We have got to the point where travel just to look and see other cultures is often not satisfying. We are looking for engagement. Many travelers want to do more than spectate.

Voluntourism

One product of such desire is voluntourism. If you haven't heard this word before, you can probably work it out. It refers to tourism with a volunteering dimension included. If you put it in your internet search engine you will be able to choose from hundreds if not thousands of options for voluntourism. You can teach English in Vietnam, do conservation work in Nepal, help protect sea turtles in Mexico or work in an orphanage in Ethiopia. The desire to engage and the ease of travel have led to the rapid expansion of the so called short-term "mission trips." "Approximately 32% of congregations in the USA sponsor international mission trips each year."[9] Many of these are short-term trips to developing countries. In the past, a short-term mission meant you would only be there for a couple of years, now it could be as short as a couple of weeks. There is quite a lot of debate of the value of these short-term trips. Some express concern that this is "drive-by mission."[10] They fear it will undermine long-term development work, crowd out local workers, divert valuable resources into looking after short-term visitors, and nurture imperialistic cultural practices. Robert Lupton in his book *Toxic Charity* gives an example that the money spent

9. Wuthnow, *Boundless Faith.*
10. Moreau, *Introducing World Missions*, 281.

by one campus ministry on their Central American mission trip to repaint an orphanage would have been enough to hire two local painters and two new full-time teachers and purchase new uniforms for every student in the school.[11] He goes on to say, "Contrary to popular belief, most missions trips and service projects do not: empower those being served, engender healthy cross-cultural relationships, improve quality of life, relieve poverty, change the lives of participants [or] increase support for long-term missions work."[12]

The growth in popularity of short-term mission trips and voluntourism reflect a world where people desire engagement. They cannot be easily dismissed. At a church I attended we started supporting the people of Vanuatu after the devastation of cyclone Pam in 2015. An immediate response of some of the young people in our church was to ask could they go there to help rebuild. They wanted personal involvement and were committed to the relational element and not just the remote experience of sending money.

Long-term partnerships are one way to ensure that compassion is both wise and beneficial. "Compassion must be guided by relationship. Love must be demonstrated with respect. And the twin principles of 'do no harm' and 'don't do for others what they can do for themselves' must be followed. . . . Local leadership, local relationship and local know how count for more than any foreign fundraising ever can."[13] The Salvation Army is ideally placed to foster partnerships. Our global connections give us networks and relationships which we can draw upon in nurturing mutual and respectful connections.

Another way to ensure these encounters are positive is to reframe the visitor as gift receiver rather than gift giver. We need to acknowledge that cross cultural engagement changes and teaches us and we are often the key recipients of the encounter. This point cannot be overstated. I have heard it suggested that we should stop using the term short-term mission trip and call them learning exchange or exposure trips. These names acknowledge the importance of the visitor as a primary, if not sole, beneficiary. Local leadership is central to dealing with local problems and long-term collaborative partnerships are the most likely to have long-term positive outcomes. Lupton offers an "oath of compassionate service" to guide Christians in short-term mission engagement:

11. Lupton, *Toxic Charity*, 5.

12. Ibid., 15.

13. Wytsma, *Pursuing Justice*, 143.

1. I will never do for others what they have (or could have) the capacity to do for themselves.

2. I will limit one-way giving to emergency situations.

3. I will seek ways to empower through employment, lending, and investing, using grants sparingly to reinforce achievements.

4. I will put the interests of the poor above my own (or organization) self-interest even when it means setting aside my own agenda.

5. I will listen closely to those I seek to help, especially to what is not being said—unspoken feelings may contain essential clues to effective service.

6. Above all, to the best of my ability, I will do no harm.[14]

Mission Snapshot: Ian and Marion Dooley, senior soldiers at the Tweed Head Corps in Australia, have been visiting and supporting Vanuatu since 2010. During one of their visits they met Lillyrose Sarilobani, from Tagabe village on the outskirts of Port Vila. Lilyrose and her husband, William, run a shelter in the village. They take in many disadvantaged children, including those abandoned by their parents. They also run a church service in their home each Sunday. The Dooleys began sending school supplies, clothes and toys for the children and others in the village. When they visited they also joined in the Sarilobani's mission. They preached God's word and hosted community meals. In 2014 Lilyrose and William became Vanuatu's first Salvation Army soldiers. In the following years, the ministry grew. In 2015 Cyclone Pam devastated Vanuatu and drew an international response from The Salvation Army. In the wake of those efforts, the ministry in that country became permanently established and officially recognized by The Salvation Army. Many people are being positively impacted by the ministry commenced by Lilyrose and William a few short years ago. Ian Dooley reflects, "We never anticipated this, we are just ordinary people going to help other ordinary people who have less than we have, and are hungry for God." *Port Vila, Vanuatu.*

---

14. Lupton, *Toxic Charity*, 128.

Engaging Online

A final way we wish to explore our global citizenship is in the online world.

Thirty years ago, as I was becoming aware of global injustices I desired to respond. So, I joined an Amnesty International letter-writing group. We met regularly to write to civic leaders all over the world in response to social injustices, like the imprisonment of prisoners of conscience, mistreatment of children and the death penalty. I am no longer a member of a letter-writing group, but I am still a member of Amnesty and in place of pen, paper and stamp, I sometimes engage in online activism. If I wish to respond to an issue I can do so online: three clicks and my work is done.

This change in my own behavior is representative of a social trend sometimes called clicktivism or more disparagingly slacktivism. Many websites outlining major social issues have integrated social media platforms into their sites so that readers can "like," "share," "tweet," or sign a petition in response to what they have read. Change.com is one of countless online activism sites offering opportunities for engagement around current issues and they rather audaciously quote the *News Daily* as saying, "It may be as simple as a click, but online activism has the power to change the world." Does it? There is certainly plenty of critique to suggest that online activism is limited at best and dangerous at worst. Its opponents suggest that online activism gives its users the sense that they are doing something, when in reality, they are doing almost nothing. In response to people using Facebook profiles to support social issues Jimmy Kimmel, a well-known US television host, reflected that "it is literally the least you can do . . . you almost did nothing, but instead you did just slightly more than nothing."[15] Further, online activism favors the digitally connected and may further marginalize those with less digital access. These are often the same group marginalized by economics and demographics. More importantly however, it may come to replace personal engagement and alienate us from the very issues with which we wish to engage. Click activism may be an expression of "excarnate mission,"[16]—the very opposite to the biblical call to incarnation as our Christian motif for living.

With that in mind though, most would still agree that there is some value in online advocacy as a tool in global social engagement. Just as Amnesty International's method of letter writing grew out of the effectiveness

---

15. Frost, *Incarnate*, 122.
16. Ibid.

of one campaign in the 1960s and has gone on to be a powerful tool ever since, so online activism has a place in the landscape of advocacy today. Here are some considerations which might help as we engage in this way.

- First, we should always be informed. What is the issue and who is reporting it? Are there alternative points of view on this issue and what are the merits of those differing arguments? Try and learn about the issue from reputable sources before clicking your way to online action.

- Second, ask yourself what are you hoping to achieve and is this action the best way to achieve it? Who does the online petition address and what outcomes does it ask for? Will your status update open debate or alienate those you wish to win over? Is the internet the best place to bring about the change you'd like to see in the world?

- Finally, click activism must be an extension of embodied activism and not a replacement. We follow a faith in which incarnation is a guiding missional principle. We follow the one who "took on flesh and blood and moved into the neighborhood" (John 1:14, The Message) and this gives us a lens through which we can assess our choices in online global social engagement.

Conclusion

This chapter is titled Being Global Citizens which might have a contemporary ring to it. However as long ago as the fourth century BCE the Greeks coined the term "cosmopolitan" from *kosmos*, meaning world and *polites*, meaning citizen. Citizens of the world. An ancient idea with very modern sensibilities. We are indeed global citizens. We are connected to others beyond our own communities and even more broadly to the wider creation. We are not solitary beings or singular cultures. In the 1600s John Donne famously said that no man is an island, entire of itself. That is truer today than when Donne penned his words or the Greeks talked of global citizenship. We encounter each other as never before. As followers of Jesus we are called to thoughtful global engagement. Our actions and interactions can create a foretaste of the kingdom of God. As we live out kingdom principles as citizens of God's good earth, we look forward to the day when we will celebrate the coming of people from all tribes, nations, languages, and people in the world which is to be.

To Learn More:

- *A Spectators Guide to World Religions: An Introduction to the Big Five,* by John Dickon.
- *From Times Square to Timbuktu: The Post-Christian West Meets the Non-Western Church,* by Wesley Granberg-Michaelson.

Toolbox:

- Search for current campaigns on The Salvation Army International Social Justice Centre (ISJC) website.
- Eat in culturally diverse places and ask the owners to explain about their country or origin to you.
- Give gifts from gift catalogues that fight injustice and poverty such as The Salvation Army, Oxfam or World Vision.
- stopthetraffik.org.

Conclusion

In the first installment of *The Lord of the Rings* movie trilogy there is a crucial scene upon which hinges the fate of the created world. A gathering of wise and learned individuals has degenerated into heated argument over who will lead a quest to destroy the one ring of power which poses a great threat to them all. As they continue to argue we see the least important, least knowledgeable and most unprepared of the group, the hobbit Frodo, rise and respond to the commotion; "I will take the ring to Mordor—though I do not know the way."

In many ways, Frodo had no idea of the implications of what he was saying, but driven by a sense of mission in response to the needs of the world he decided to act. Naive and ignorant words, perhaps, but this was a heart-felt response born of a desire to make a difference. Frodo saw great need and decided he must do something about it. Many others would choose to run the other way.

Throughout the pages of this book we have outlined the story of the mission of God and also a challenge to be people who partner with God in mission. There is always more to know. We may never feel we really have the skills or capacity we need to actually make a difference. The resultant temptation is to wait and watch, and hope that someone else will take up the mantle of mission. However, mission is not a spectator sport. It is not something we can read and talk about alone. Mission is at the core of what it means to be a person of faith in Jesus and so God lovingly invites us to partner in that work. The church is only ever truly the church as it is active in mission. Our hearts and prayers echo with the refrain "May your kingdom come on earth as it is in heaven."

Like Frodo we have an opportunity to rise to the challenge of meaningful mission. Our ignorance of the intricacies and finer points of the *missio Dei* need not prevent our involvement. We don't have to have it all mapped out and know the way. We are collaborators in the mission of the kingdom of God and so we can follow, and learn, and grow as we partner in God's kingdom work. It is time for us to say: "I will build the kingdom of God on earth as in heaven—though I do not know the way." God knows. We join the Godhead in a millennia old partnership of transforming work. Many chapters of this unfolding story have already been written, and we are called to contribute to the next chapter. What story will your life write?

As this book ends I trust the next steps are clear enough even though none of us are experts. Think mission, yes. Live mission, most definitely yes! May we be people who respond to the transformational work of God in our lives by seeking transformation for all creatures and all of creation. Go and be blessed in order to be agents of God's blessing.

Bibliography

Aboagye-Mensah, Robert. "The World Our Parish: Christian Mission and the Wesleyan Heritage in a Ghanian Context." In *World Mission in the Wesleyan Spirit*, edited by Darrell L. Whiteman et al., 53–61. Franklin, TN: Providence House, 2009.

Adeney, Frances. *Graceful Evangelism: Christian Witness in a Complex World*. Grand Rapids: Baker, 2010.

Aikman, David. "Suffocating the Faithful: Will the Last Middle East Church Leader Be Sure to Turn Off the Lights?" *Christianity Today* 51 (2007) 58.

Alfred, Charlotte. "What History Can Teach Us about the Worst Refugee Crisis since WWII." *Huffington Post*, 9 December 2015. http://www.huffingtonpost.com.au/entry/alexander-betts-refugees-wwii_55f30f7ce4b077ca094edaec?section=australia&adsSiteOverride=au.

Anderson, Gerald H. "Prevenient Grace in World Mission." In *World Mission in the Wesleyan Spirit*, edited by Darrell L. Whiteman et al., 34–52. Franklin, TN: Providence House, 2009.

———. "Theology of Religions and Missiology: A Time of Testing." In *The Good News of the Kingdom: Mission Theology for the Third Millennium*, edited by Charles Van Engen et al., 200–208. Maryknoll: Orbis, 1993.

Bahnson, Fred, and Norman Wirzba. *Making Peace with the Land: God's Call to Reconcile with Creation*. Downers Grove: InterVarsity, 2012.

Bartholomew, Craig, and Michael Goheen. *The Drama of Scripture: Finding Our Place in the Biblical Story*. Grand Rapids: Baker, 2014.

Bauckham, Richard. "Mission as Hermeneutic." Lecture given at Cambridge. http://richardbauckham.co.uk/uploads/Accessible/Mission%20as%20Hermeneutic.pdf.

Bediako, Kwame. *Christianity in Africa: The Renewal of Non-Western religion*. New York: Orbis, 1997.

Bellofatto Gina A., and Todd M. Johnson. "Key Findings of Christianity in Its Global Context, 1970–2020." *International Bulletin of Missionary Research* 37 (2013) 157–64.

Bennett, Christi-An C. "Theological Foundations of Wesleyan Missiology in Historical Perspective." *Mediator: A Journal of Holiness Theology for Asia-Pacific Contexts* 3 (2002) 67–78.

Berger, Arthur. "The Day the World Changed: A Pomo Primer." *Society* 49 (2012) 317–22.

Block, Peter, et al. *An Other Kingdom: Departing the Consumer Culture*. Hoboken, NJ: Wiley, 2016.

Boff, Leonardo, and Clodovis Boff. *Introducing Liberation Theology*. Translated by Paul Burns. New York: Orbis, 2001.

Bolton, Barbara. *Booth's Drum: The Salvation Army in Australia 1880–1980*. Sydney: Hodder & Stoughton, 1980.

Booth, William. "O Boundless Salvation." In *The Songbook of The Salvation Army*. London: CPI, 2015.

———. "Salvation for Both Worlds." *All the World* (Salvation Army magazine), January 1889, 1–6.

Bosch, David. "Reflections on Biblical Models of Mission." In *Toward the Twenty-First Century in Christian Mission: Essays in Honor of Gerald H. Anderson*, edited by James Phillips et al., 175–92. Grand Rapids: Eerdmans. 1993.

———. *Transforming Mission: Paradigm Shifts in Theology of Mission*. New York: Orbis, 1991.

———. *Witness to the World: The Christian Mission in Theological Perspective*. Atlanta: John Knox, 1980.

Bright, John. *The Kingdom of God*. Nashville: Abingdon, 1981.

Brown, Callum G. *The Death of Christian Britain: Understanding Secularisation, 1800–2000*. 2nd ed. London: Routledge, 2009.

Brueggemann, Walter. *The Land: Place as Gift, Promise and Challenge in Biblical Faith*. Philadelphia: Fortress, 1997.

———. *Reverberations of Faith: A Theological Handbook of Old Testament Themes*. Louisville: Westminster John Knox, 2002.

Burke, Donald. "The Wesleyan View of Salvation and Social Involvement." In *Creed and Deed: Toward a Christian Theology of Social Services in the Salvation Army*, edited by John. D. Waldron, 2–9. Canada: Salvation Army, 1986.

Burns, Alan. *Founding Vision for a Future Army: Spiritual Renewal and Mission in The Salvation Army*. London: Crest, 2012.

Cherry, Constance. *The Worship Architect: A Blueprint for Designing Culturally Relevant and Biblically Faithful Services*. Grand Rapids: Baker Academic, 2010.

Church of England General Synod. *Mission Shaped Church: Church Planting and Fresh Expressions of Church in a Changing Context*. London: Church House, 2004.

Cleary, John. "Boundless Salvation: An Historical Perspective on the Theology of Salvationist Mission." Report for The Salvation Army. Melbourne, 2001.

Cox, Harvey. *God's Revolution and Man's Responsibility*. Valley Forge, PA: Judson, 1965.

Davies-Kildea, Jason. "Unwrapping Our Bounded Salvation." In *Thought Matters: Soul Salvation Whole Salvation; Towards a Theology of Social Justice*. Thought Matters Papers. Melbourne: Salvation Army, 2011.

Dawn, Marva. "Worship to Form a Missional Community." *Direction* 28 (1999) 139–52.

Dayton, Donald W. "Good News to the Poor: The Methodist Experience after Wesley." In *The Portion of the Poor: Good News to the Poor in the Wesleyan Tradition*, edited by Douglas M. Meeks, 65–96. Nashville: Abingdon, 1995.

Dennis, Margo G. "In Her Own Right: Women Officers and Equality in the Salvation Army." Masters diss., Deakin University, Victoria, 1998.

DeYmaz, Mark. *Building a Healthy Multi-ethnic Church: Mandate, Commitments and Practices of a Diverse Congregation*. San Francisco: Jossey-Bass, 2007.

DeYmaz, Mark, and Harry Li. *Ethnic Blends: Mixing Diversity into Your Local Church*. Grand Rapids: Zondervan, 2010.

Diab, Issa. "Middle Eastern Christianity: Yesterday, Today, and Tomorrow." *International Congregational Journal* 12 (2013) 35–54.

Dickson, John. *Humilitas: A Lost Key to Life, Love and Leadership.* Grand Rapids: Zondervan, 2011.

———. *A Spectators Guide to World Religions: An Introduction to the Big Five.* Oxford: Lion, 2008.

Drane, John. *The McDonalization of the Church: Spirituality, Creativity and the Future of the Church.* London: Darton, 2005.

———. *What Is the New Age Still Saying to the Church?* London: HarperCollins, 1999.

Dumbrell, William J. *Covenant and Creation: An Old Testament Covenantal Theology.* Milton Keys: Paternoster, 1984.

Eason, Andrew Mark. *Women in God's Army: Gender and Equality in the Early Salvation Army.* Studies in Women and Religion. Canada: Wilfrid Laurier University Press, 2003.

Easum, William M. *Dancing with Dinosaurs.* Nashville: Abingdon, 1993.

Eichrodt, Walther. *Theology of the Old Testament.* Vol. 2. Philadelphia: Westminster, 1967.

Emerton, Claire. "Flawed Folklore." In *Hidden Treasure: Valuing Women in The Salvation Army*, edited by Leanne Ruthven, 56–65. Melbourne: Salvo, 2014.

Escobar, Samuel. *The New Global Mission: The Gospel from Everywhere to Everyone.* Downers Grove: InterVarsity, 2003.

Escott, Phillip. "Church Growth Theories and The Salvation Army in the United Kingdom." PhD Diss., University of Stirling, 1996.

Fleming, Dean. *Recovering the Full Mission of God: A Biblical Perspective on Being, Doing and Telling.* Downers Grove: InterVarsity, 2013.

Foster, Richard J. *Celebration of Discipline: The Path to Spiritual Growth.* London: Hodder & Stoughton, 1980.

Fowler, James. *Stages of Faith: The Psychology of Human Development.* New York: HarperCollins, 1995.

Fretheim, Terence E. *The Suffering of God: An Old Testament Perspective.* Philadelphia: Fortress, 1984.

Frost, Michael. *Exiles: Living Missionally in a Post-Christian Culture.* Peabody: Hendrickson, 2006.

———. *Incarnate: The Body of Christ in an Age of Disengagement.* Downers Grove: InterVarsity, 2014.

———. *The Road to Missional.* Grand Rapids: Baker, 2011.

———. *Surprise the World: The Five Habits of Highly Missional People.* Colorado Springs: NavPress, 2016.

Frost, Michael, and Alan Hirsch. *The Shaping of Things to Come: Innovation and Mission for the 21st-Century.* Grand Rapids: Baker, 2013.

Gallagher, Vincent. *True Cost of Low Prices: The Violence of Globalization.* Maryknoll: Orbis, 2006.

Gledhill, Ruth. "New Figures Reveal Massive Decline in Religious Affiliation." *Christianity Today*, October 17, 2014. http://www.christiantoday.com/article/exclusive.new. figures.reveal.massive.decline.in.religious.affiliation/41799.htm.

Goheen, Michael W. *Introducing Christian Mission Today: Scripture, History, and Issues.* Downers Grove: InterVarsity, 2014.

———. *A Light to the Nations: The Missional Church and the Biblical Story.* Grand Rapids: Baker, 2011.

———. "Nourishing Our Missional Identity: Worship and the Mission of God's People." In *In Praise of Worship: An Exploration of Text and Practice*, edited by David J. Cohen et al., 32–53. Eugene, OR: Wipf & Stock, 2010.

Granberg-Michaelson, Wesley. *From Times Square to Timbuktu: The Post-Christian West Meets the Non-Western Church*. Grand Rapids: Eerdmans, 2013.

———. "Think Christianity Is Dying? No, Christianity Is Shifting Dramatically." *Washington Post*, May 20, 2015. https://www.washingtonpost.com/news/acts-of-faith/wp/2015/05/20/think-christianity-is-dying-no-christianity-is-shifting-dramatically.

Green, Michael. *Evangelism in the Early Church*. Grand Rapids: Eerdmans, 2003.

Green, Roger. *War on Two Fronts: The Redemptive Theology of William Booth*. Atlanta: Salvation Army, 1989.

Greenaway, Roger, and Timothy Monsma. *Cities: Missions' New Frontier*. Grand Rapids: Baker, 2000.

Guder, Darrell L., ed. *Missional Church: A Vision for the Sending of the Church in North America*. Grand Rapids: Eerdmans, 1998.

Haley Barton, Ruth. *Sacred Rhythms: Arranging Our Lives for Spiritual Transformation*. Downers Grove: InterVarsity, 2006.

Hall, Bob, and Alan Jamieson. "The Interplay of Mission and Worship: A Doxological View." *Australian Journal of Mission Studies* 7 (2013) 48–56.

Halliday, Kris. "Making Sense of Scripture and The Salvation Army as a Gay Person Called to Officership." In *Honour God with Your Body*, edited by David Janssen and Christina Tyson, 117–28. Melbourne: Salvation Army, 2015.

Hammond, Kim, and Darren Cronshaw. *Sentness: Six Postures of Missional Christians*. Downers Grove: InterVarsity, 2014.

Harnack, Adolf. *The Mission and Expansion of Christianity in the First Three Centuries*. Vol. 1. Translated by James Moffat. New York: Harper, 2012.

Hattersley, Roy. *Blood and Fire: William and Catherine Booth and Their Salvation Army*. London: Abacus, 2000.

Helland, Roger, and Leonard Hjalmarson. *Missional Spirituality: Embodying God's Love from the Inside Out*. Downers Grove: InterVarsity, 2011.

Hiatt, R. Jeffrey. "John Wesley's Approach to Mission." *Asbury Journal* 68 (2013) 108–24.

Hill, Graham. *Salt, Light and a City: Introducing Missional Ecclesiology*. Eugene, OR: Wipf & Stock, 2012.

Hirsch, Alan. *The Forgotten Ways: Reactivating the Missional Church*. Grand Rapids: Brazos, 2006.

Hogg, William R. H. *Ecumenical Foundations: A History of the International Missionary Council and Its Nineteenth Century Background*. New York: Harper, 1952.

Inglis, Kenneth. *Churches and the Working Classes in Victorian England*. London: Routledge, 1963.

Jacobsen, Douglas. *The World's Christians: Who They Are, Where They Are, and How They Got There*. Chichester: Wiley-Blackwell, 2011.

Janin, Hunt, and Ursula Carlson. *Mercenaries in Medieval and Renaissance Europe*. Jefferson, NC: McFarland, 2013.

Janssen, David, and Christina Tyson, eds. *Honour God with Your Body: A Christian View of Human Sexuality*. Melbourne: Salvation Army, 2015.

Jenkins, Philip. *The Next Christendom: The Coming Global Christianity*. New York: Oxford University Press, 2011.

Johnson, Todd M. *Atlas of Global Christianity, 1910–2010*. Edinburgh: Edinburgh University Press, 2009.

Johnson, Todd. M, et al. "Christianity 2015: Religious Diversity and Personal Contact." *International Bulletin of Missionary Research* 39 (2015) 28–29.

Keller, Timothy. *Generous Justice: How God's Grace Makes Us Just*. New York: Dutton, 2010.

———. "Our New Global Culture: Ministry in Urban Centers." White paper. New York, 2010. http://churchplants.com/free-downloads/8564-free-ebooklet-our-new-global-culture-ministry-urban-centers-timothy-keller.html.

Kennedy, John F. "Address before the Canadian Parliament in Ottawa." May 17, 1961. http://www.presidency.ucsb.edu/ws/?pid=8136.

Kim, Elijah J. F. *The Rise of the Global South: The Decline of Western Christendom and the Rise of Majority World Christianity*. Eugene, OR: Wipf & Stock, 2012.

King, Martin Luther, Jr. *Strength to Love*. London: Collins, 1969.

Kirk, J. Andrew. *What Is Mission? Theological Explorations*. London: Darton, Longman and Todd, 1999.

Kluth, Brian. "40 Day Spiritual Journey to a More Generous Life." http://www.kluth.org/book.pdf.

Köstenberger, Andreas, and Peter O'Brien. *Salvation to the Ends of the Earth: A Biblical Theology of Mission*. Downers Grove: InterVarsity, 2001.

Kozhuharov, Valentin. "Christian Mission in Eastern Europe." *International Bulletin of Missionary* 37 (2013) 73–76.

Kreider, Alan, and Eleanor Kreider. *Worship and Mission after Christendom*. Harrisonburg: Herald, 2011.

Lausanne Movement. "Lausanne Global Consultation on Creation Care and the Gospel: Call to Action." St. Ann, Jamaica, November 2012. https://www.lausanne.org/content/statement/creation-care-call-to-action.

———. "Manila Manifesto." July 20, 1989. http://www.lausanne.org/en/documents/manila-manifesto.html.

Leith, John H., ed. *Creeds of the Churches: A Reader in Christian Doctrine, from the Bible to Present*. 3rd ed. Louisville: John Knox, 1982.

Lewis, C. S. *Letters to an American Lady*. Grand Rapids: Eerdmans, 1967.

———. *Mere Christianity*. New York: HarperOne, 1980.

———. *The Weight of Glory*. San Francisco: HarperOne, 2001.

Lupton, Robert. *Toxic Charity: How Churches and Charities Hurt Those They Help (and How to Reverse It)*. New York: HaperOne, 2011.

Luther, Martin. *Luther's Works*. Edited by Jaroslay Pelikan and Helmut T. Lehmann. Vol. 53. Fortress, 1957. http://fortresspress.com/product/luthers-works-digital-download.

Lyon, David. *Jesus in Disneyland*. Cambridge: Polity, 2000.

MacMillan, Christine, et al. *When Justice Is the Measure*. Toronto: Salvation Army, 2014.

Mandryk, Jason. *Operation World: The Definitive Prayer Guide to Every Nation*. 7th ed. Downers Grove: InterVarsity, 2010.

Mason, Michael, et al. *The Spirit of Generation Y: Young People's Spirituality in a Changing Australia*. Victoria: Garratt, 2007.

McCrindle, Mark. "A Demographic Snapshot of Christianity and Church Attenders in Australia." April 18, 2014. http://mccrindle.com.au/the-mccrindle-blog/a-demographic-snapshot-of-christianity-and-church-attenders-in-australia.

McLaren, Brian. *More Ready than You Realize: Evangelism as Dance in the Postmodern Matrix*. Grand Rapids: Zondervan, 2002.

McNeal, Reggie. *Kingdom Come: Why We Must Give Up Our Obsession with Fixing the Church and What We Should Do Instead*. Carol Stream, IL: Tyndale, 2015.

———. *Missional Renaissance: Changing the Scorecard for the Church*. San Francisco: Jossey-Bass, 2009.

Meyers, Ruth A. *Missional Worship, Worshipful Mission: Gathering as God's People, Going Out in God's Name*. Grand Rapids: Eerdmans, 2014.

Micah Network. "Integral Mission." http://www.micahnetwork.org/integral-mission.

Michel, Thomas F. *Christian View of Islam: Essays on Dialogue*. Maryknoll: Orbis, 2010.

Middleton, J. Richard. "The Liberating Image? Interpreting the Imago Dei in Context." *Christian Scholars Review* 24 (1994) 8–25.

Miller, Andy, III. *Holistic Hospitality: A Bridge to a Future Army*. Atlanta: Salvation Army, 2015.

Moltmann, Jürgen. *The Church in the Power of the Spirit: A Contribution to Messianic Ecclesiology*. London: SCM, 1977.

Moreau, Scott, et al. *Introducing World Missions: A Biblical, Historical and Practical Survey*. Grand Rapids: Baker, 2004.

Moss, Rowland. *The Earth in Our Hands*. Leicester: InterVarsity, 1928.

Motyer, J. Alec. *The Prophecy of Isaiah: An Introduction and Commentary*. Downers Grove: InterVarsity, 1993.

Muck, Terry, and Frances S. Adeney. *Christianity Encountering World Religions*. Grand Rapids: Baker, 2009.

Munn, Janet. *Theory and Practice of Gender Equality in The Salvation Army*. Ashland, OH: Gracednotes, 2015.

Munn, Nealson, and David Collinson. *Insane*. Melbourne: Salvo, 2007.

Murdoch, Norman H. *Origins of the Salvation Army*. Knoxville: University of Tennessee Press, 1994.

Murray, Stuart. *Post Christendom: Church and Mission in a Strange New World*. Milton Keys: Paternoster, 2004.

Needham, Phil. *Community in Mission: A Salvationist Ecclesiology*. St Albans: Campfield, 1987.

———. "Toward a Re-integration of the Salvationist Mission." In *Creed and Deed: Toward a Christian Theology of Social Services in the Salvation Army*, edited by John D. Waldron, 123–58. Toronto: Salvation Army, 1986.

Neill, Stephen. *A History of Christian Missions*. London: Penguin, 1990.

Nouwen, Henri. *Spiritual Formation: Following the Movements of the Spirit*. New York: HarperOne, 2010.

Oduro, Thomas A. "Arise, Walk through the Length and Breadth of the Land: Missionary Concepts and Strategies of African Independent Churches." *International Bulletin of Missionary Research* 38 (2014) 86–89.

Ortberg, John, and Pam Howell. "Can You Engage Both Heart and Mind? The Power of Connecting the Whole Self with the Holy God." *Leadership* 20 (1999) http://www.christianitytoday.com/pastors/1999/spring/9l2o32.html.

Ott, Craig, et al. *Encountering Theology of Mission: Biblical Foundations, Historical Development and Contemporary Issues*. Grand Rapids: Baker Academic, 2010.

Padilla, C. Rene. "A New Ecclesiology in Latin America." *International Bulletin of Missionary Research* 11 (1987) 156–64.

Pennington, Brian K. *Was Hinduism Invented? Britons, Indians, and the Colonial Construction*. Oxford: Oxford University Press, 2005.

Peterson, Eugene H. *A Long Obedience in the Same Direction: Discipleship in an Instant Society*. 2nd ed. Downers Grove: InterVarsity, 2000.

Pierce, Gregory. *The Mass Is Never Ended: Rediscovering our Mission to Transform the World*. Notre Dame: Ave Maria, 2007.

Plantinga, Corneluis, Jr. *Not the Way It's Supposed to Be: A Breviary of Sin*. Grand Rapids: Eerdmans, 1995.

Pohl, Christine D. "Hospitality, a Practice and a Way of Life." *Vision* 3 (2002) 34–43.

Pope, M. "Preaching to the Birds: The Mission of the Church to the Creation." Tinsley Annual Lecture, Morling College, May 2013. With Mick Pope. http://www.morlingcollege.com/wp-content/uploads/2013%20Annual%20Lecture%20Booklet.pdf.

Radner, Ephraim. "Anglicanism on Its Knees." *First Things: A Monthly Journal of Religion & Public Life: Religion and Philosophy Collection* 243 (2014) 45–50.

Ramachandra, Vinoth. *Gods That Fail: Modern Idolatry and Christian Mission*. Downers Grove: InterVarsity, 1997.

Read, John. *Catherine Booth: Laying the Theological Foundations of a Radical Movement*. Eugene, OR: Pickwick, 2013.

Rendell, Ruth. "We Have Caught the Vision Splendid." Hymn 938 in *The Songbook of The Salvation Army*. London: CPI, 2015.

Robinson, Marilynne. *Gilead*. New York: Picador, 2004.

Salvation Army. *The Salvation Army Handbook of Doctrine*. London: Salvation, 2010.

———. *The Salvation Army in the Body of Christ: An Ecclesiological Statement*. London: Salvation, 2008.

Sandall, Robert. *The History of the Salvation Army*. Vol. 2. London: Nelson, 1950.

Savage, Sara B., et al. *Making Sense of Generation Y: The World View of 15 to 25 Year-Olds*. London: Church House, 2006.

Scazzero, Peter. *Emotionally Healthy Spirituality: Unleash a Revolution in Your Life in Christ*. Nashville: Nelson, 2006.

Schmit, Clayton J. *Sent and Gathered: A Worship Manual for the Missional Church*. Grand Rapids: Baker, 2009.

Schultz, Thom, and Joani Schultz. *Why Nobody Wants to Go to Church Anymore*. Colorado: Group, 2013.

Seaman, Matthew. "Dark Green Religion and the Wesleyan Tradition: Harmony and Dissonance." *Wesleyan Theological Journal* 48 (2013) 135–48.

———. "Recapturing a Salvationist Vision for All the Earth." In *Thought Matters: Vision for the Lost or a Lost Vision? William Booth's Legacy 100 Years On*. Melbourne: Salvation Army, 2013.

Sittser, Gerald L. *Water from a Deep Well: Christian Spirituality from Early Martyrs to Modern Missionaries*. Downers Grove: InterVarsity, 2007.

Snyder, Howard A. "The Missional Flavor of John Wesley's Theology" In *World Mission in the Wesleyan Spirit*, edited by Darrell L. Whiteman et al., 62–73. Franklin, TN: Providence House, 2009.

———. *Yes in Christ: Wesleyan Reflections on Gospel, Mission, and Culture*. Toronto: Clements, 2010.

Sölle, Dorothee. *The Strength of the Weak: Toward a Christian Feminist Identity*. Philadelphia: Westminster, 1984.

Stackhouse, John. "Why Does God Allow So Much Evil in the World?" February 5, 2015. http://wonderingfair.com/2015/02/05/why-does-god-allow-so-much-evil-in-the-world.

Stark, Rodney. *The Rise of Christianity: How the Obscure, Marginal Jesus Movement Became the Dominant Religious Force in the Western World in a Few Centuries.* San Francisco: Princeton University Press, 1996.

Stone, Bryan. *Evangelism after Christendom: The Theology and Practice of Christian Witness.* Grand Rapids: Brazos, 2007.

Sweet, Leonard. *SoulTsunami: Sink or Swim in New Millennium Culture.* Grand Rapids: Zondervan, 1999.

Tacey, David. *The Spirituality Revolution: The Emergence of Contemporary Spirituality.* Sydney: HarperCollins, 2003.

Tarnas, Richard. *The Passion of the Western Mind: Understanding the Ideas That Have Shaped Our World View.* New York: Ballantine, 1991.

Taylor, Steve. *The Out of Bounds Church: Learning to Create a Community of Faith in a Culture of Change.* Grand Rapids: Zondervan, 2005.

Thielicke, Helmut. *How Modern Should Theology Be?* Philadelphia: Fortress, 1969.

United Nations, Department of Economic and Social Affairs, Population Division. "World Urbanization Prospects: The 2014 Revision." https://esa.un.org/unpd/wup/publications/files/wup2014-highlights.pdf.

Uniting Church in Australia. *Uniting in Worship: Leaders Book.* Melbourne: Uniting Church, 1988.

Van Gelder, Craig, and Dwight J. Zscheile. *The Missional Church in Perspective: Mapping Trends and Shaping the Conversation.* Grand Rapids: Baker, 2011.

Volf, Mirsolav. *After Our Likeness: The Church as the Image of the Trinity.* Sacra Doctrina: Christian Theology for a Postmodern Age. Grand Rapids: Eerdmans, 1997.

———. *Exclusion and Embrace: A Theological Exploration of Identity, Otherness and Reconciliation.* Nashville: Abingdon, 1996.

Walls, Andrew. "From Christendom to World Christianity: Missions and the Demographic Transformation of the Church." *Princeton Seminary Bulletin* 22 (2001) 306–30.

———. "The Legacy of David Livingstone." *International Bulletin of Missionary Research* 11 (1987) 125–28.

———. *The Missionary Movement in Christian History: Studies in Transmission of Faith.* New York: Orbis, 1996.

Webber, Robert. *Ancient-Future Evangelism: Making Your Church a Faith-Forming Community.* Grand Rapids: Baker, 2007.

———. *Ancient-Future Worship: Proclaiming and Enacting God's Narrative.* Grand Rapids: Baker, 2008.

———. *The Divine Embrace: Recovering the Passionate Spiritual Life.* Grand Rapids: Baker, 2006.

Wesley, John. *The Works of John Wesley.* Vol. 14. Grand Rapids: Zondervan, 1872.

West, Andrew. "A Leap of Faith for Church and State." *Sydney Morning Herald*, 22 April 2011. http://www.smh.com.au/nsw/a-leap-of-faith-for-church-and-state-20110421-1dqoo.html#ixzz3nwjmffdU.

White, James Emery. *The Rise of the Nones: Understanding and Reaching the Religiously Unaffiliated.* Grand Rapids: Baker, 2014.

White, Lynn. "The Historical Roots of Our Ecological Crisis." *Science* 155 (1967) 1203–7.

Willard, Dallas. *The Divine Conspiracy: Rediscovering Our Hidden Life in God*. San Fransisco: Harper Collins, 1998.

———. *The Great Omission: Reclaiming Jesus's Essential Teachings on Discipleship*. San Francisco: HarperSanFrancisco, 2006.

Woo, Rodney M. *The Color of Church: A Biblical and Practical Paradigm for Multiracial Churches*. Nashville: B&H Academic, 2009.

World Council of Churches. "Constitution and Rules of the World Council of Churches." October 30, 2013. https://www.oikoumene.org/en/resources/documents/assembly/2013-busan/adopted-documents-statements/wcc-constitution-and-rules.

Wright, Christopher J. H. *The Mission of God: Unlocking the Bible's Grand Narrative*. Nottingham: InterVarsity, 2006.

———. *The Mission of God's People: A Biblical Theology of the Church's Mission*. Grand Rapids: Zondervan, 2010.

———. *Old Testament Ethics for the People of God*. Leicester: InterVarsity, 2004.

———. "Truth with a Mission: Reading All Scriptures Missiologically." In *Text & Task: Scripture & Mission*, edited by Michael Parsons, 140–56. Milton Keynes: Paternoster, 2012.

Wright, N.T. "Freedom and Framework, Spirit and Truth: Recovering Biblical Worship." *Studia Liturgica* 32 (2002) 176–95.

———. *Simply Good News: Why the Gospel Is News and What Makes It Good*. New York: HarperOne, 2015

———. *Surprised by Hope: Rethinking Heaven, the Resurrection, and the Mission of the Church*. New York: HarperOne, 2008.

Wuthnow, R. *Boundless Faith: The Global Outreach of American Churches*. Berkeley: University of California Press, 2009.

Wytsma, Ken. *Pursuing Justice: The Call to Live & Die for Bigger Things*. Nashville: Nelson, 2013.

Yad Vashem. "Chiune Sempo Sugihara, Japan." http://www.yadvashem.org/righteous/stories/sugihara.

Yancey, Philip. "God at Large: A Look around the Globe Reveals a God as Big as We Want Him to Be." *Christianity Today* 45 (2001) 135–36.

———. *The Jesus I Never Knew*. Grand Rapids: Zondervan, 1995.

———. *What's So Amazing about Grace?* Grand Rapids: Zondervan, 1997.

Yuill, Chick. *Leadership on the Axis of Change*. Alexandria: Salvation Army, 2003.

Index